Contents:

C000245698

Introduction

INTRODUCTION

Football clubs have been touring ever since football clubs existed. At one end of the scale a tour can be the local pub team playing a couple of games against another boozer in Blackpool – accompanied, of course, by two days on the lash. At the other end of the scale, Manchester United can visit Japan in a media frenzied sales pitch aimed at boosting the coffers of the PLC by reaching the holy grail that is the Far East market. Most of the others fall somewhere in between.

It may be difficult, therefore, to appreciate just what happened to Crook Town of The Northern League on their post season tour in 1976. You see, if you were to place it on the scale between 'boozer in Blackpool' and Man United in Japan', it would be placed very close to the oriental option. I came across the story when researching 'One Dead Ref and a Box of Kippers' and decided I had to find out more about what sounded like an incredible adventure.

'Can You Get Bobby Charlton?' is the story of the India Tour pieced together from the memories of eight men associated with the club and the tour, plus newspaper reports of the time. Inevitably, aspects of the recall from 1976 have dimmed slightly and I have had to play referee with some of the conflicting recollections. And while the conversations recorded in the book cannot possibly be the exact words that were spoken, they are based on the tales and anecdotes as related faithfully to me, with a little bit of artistic licence thrown in. But even if the odd detail may be argued over by some of the tourists, I hope the book conveys a sense of how the tour developed into the astonishing phenomenon that it became. Despite the name on the title and the presence of one or two other well-known names from the football world, this is essentially the true story of how Crook Town found themselves at the centre of a popular, media, political and social whirlwind that swept across north-east India and made national celebrities of a group of unknown players.

Trip of a lifetime? You bet it was!

Crook, February 2003 (Part I)

A week before our meeting, I sampled the inimitable Dr. Banerjee by way of the telephone. Having arrived back home from a very agreeable evening in the company of friends I was handed a note by our baby sitter indicating that the doctor had called me.

"Mind you," warned my exhausted messenger, "you'll never get off the phone. He could talk for England... well, India."

He was up late watching the cricket world cup on Sky television so would be more than happy to take my return call, no matter how late it was. I was feeling a little bloated after a mammoth meal that centred around a giant Yorkshire pudding filled with the most tender lamb and wasn't sure if I was up to polite chat with a stranger. But this was the call I'd been hoping for since I'd first stumbled across the story of 'The India Trip' some months earlier.

It was around midnight, an hour at which most people would be nervous about hearing a telephone ring, fearing a family crisis or call-out from work and following several pints of decent ale I was seriously concerned about sounding incoherent. I needn't have worried; I hardly had the chance to say anything. I had been trying to contact the good doctor for some weeks so I was delighted at receiving the call and punched in the numbers with some urgency lest India had been bowled out and he had retired hurt to bed.

"Hello. Dr. Banerjee here."

"Ah. Dr. Banerjee. It's Steven Chaytor – you called me earlier. I have been...."

"Oh, yes, yes, I spoke to your mother. She was looking after your children. We are watching the cricket. This is normal for me. You want to talk about Crook Town...the India tour. You have come to the right man. I can tell you everything. The others will tell you some things but only I can tell you exactly what happened. My sons were also on the tour. They are both doctors now. One specialises in lung cancer and the other specialises in orthopaedic surgery. We have just returned from Calcutta. My son has been married. I was just talking to my nephew on the phone in Canada to pass on all the family news and also I called Australia...."

"Blimey, Dr. Banerjee. You must have a helluva phone bill."

"Oh yes. Two thousand pounds a quarter. My accountant says that if I get rid of the bloody phone I'll be a rich man. I phone my family every day. I speak to my father in Calcutta every day. You know there are only two people who truly love you; your mother and father. And God of course. But he's not on earth so he doesn't count. So you must be good to them and respect them. But I'm not interested in money. If I can save lives, that's all I'm interested in."

"Oh, I thought you were retired."

"Well, I am. But I still do the odd surgery.."

"To keep your hand in, eh?"

"Well, I have a lot of knowledge and experience."

"What's your first name Dr. Banerjee?"

"It's Arun. That's A..R..U..N. Arun Banerjee."

"Would you like me to call you Arun or Dr. Banerjee?"

"Mmm...Dr. Banerjee."

And so continued my introduction to the man who would be the catalyst for the story I was attempting to uncover. It was a conversation of breathtaking pace and of the most unexpected twists and turns. The experience was not unlike skiing downhill...off-piste...blindfold. I don't recall ever feeling quite so exhilarated after a simple phone call. Usually when you are speaking to someone on the telephone you gradually gain a mental picture of what they might look like. In this case there wasn't time.

"So, I'll meet you next week then, Dr. Banerjee."

"Yes, yes. That will be fine. On Sunday. What time do you have your Sunday lunch? Do you have a nice roast...beef or lamb? You can't miss Sunday lunch."

"Oh, that's not a problem. We usually eat late...chicken as a matter of fact."

"I always have my Sunday dinner at lunch time...with a glass of wine. My wife is a very good cook. She spoils me. We believe in the tradition...when you are in Rome. She makes wonderful Yorkshire puddings with a special adaptation. Of course, there is no beef in this house. We also enjoy chicken."

We exchange further views on the merits of the great English Sunday meal before I venture to request directions to the Banerjee home. After giving me very detailed instructions, including optional routes from Bishop Auckland and Durham, he suggests that, if I'm lost, anyone will be able to tell me the way.

"Oh, you just ask for the doctor's house. Everyone knows the doctor's house. Only medically trained people have ever lived in this house. Everyone knows this."

I left the conversation in little doubt that most people would indeed know where the good doctor lives. I simply can't imagine anyone from the area not knowing him.

Sunday the 23rd of February was the sort of dank and drizzly day that is a speciality of the second month. It didn't rain but it was wet. It wasn't dark but you needed your headlights. It wasn't cold but you had to wear a coat. The journey from Sedgefield to Crook appeared to be in monochrome. I half expected to be able to adjust my aerial and get a better picture through my windscreen. Nevertheless, armed with a few prepared questions, some 'topics for discussion' and my note book, I took the Bishop Auckland option. Picking my way through a deserted town centre one-way system in the famous 'seat of the Prince Bishops', the route took me across the impressive viaduct spanning Newton Cap high above the wandering river Wear with its plaque celebrating the fact that it was officially opened by the Rt. Hon. Derek Foster MP. Strange custom that – members of parliament opening bridges and roads. Why? I then headed straight towards Crook with a certain amount of concern over how I could capture the doctor's conversation without the aid of a tape recorder. I already knew....this man could talk.

Crook is an ex coal-mining town in Co. Durham. But then again, most towns and villages to the centre and east of the county answer to that description. However, Crook could boast twenty-six 'pits' in and around it during the peak years of the mid-nineteenth century and it prospered as a small industrial town until the demise of mining by the 1960's. Nowadays, in common with so many other communities with the same background, it is attempting to re-define itself and regenerate a struggling economy. It's neat, it's tidy. It has a certain charm. It is also home to an amateur football team playing in the Northern League that once toured India playing to crowds of over 100,000 at The Eden Gardens test cricket ground, something no other football club in the world has achieved. Despite the many and varied attractions of Crook the town, it was this fact alone that brought me to the doorstep of Dr. Arun Banerjee on 23rd February 2003.

After three firm raps on the door, I was greeted by a small, trim man in a crisp, pastel shirt and appropriately matching tie. His head was completely bereft of hair.

"Ah, we've been expecting you. Come in. Come in."

We entered a spacious sitting room with four low, green chairs around a square coffee table. The space was cheerfully uncluttered but decorated with strategically placed ornaments and a scene from the epic Mahabharata that dominated the room. A large music collection hinted at a room used for relaxation and numerous sporting trophies indicated a family of some athletic achievement.

"Sit down. Sit down. So you want to talk about The India tour? Have you spoken to anyone else yet?"

"No. Well, yes actually. I spoke to Michael Manual…you know, he wrote the history of Crook town. I'd heard about the story from Gordon Jones who I'd interviewed a few months ago for another book. It sounded a fascinating story and it seemed that you were a key figure in making it happen."

"Ah, yes. It was my contacts in India. Have you spoken to Ronnie James? You must speak to Ronnie."

"So it was you and Ronnie who organised the trip, then?"

"Well, I would say that I decided what had to be done and Ronnie did much of the work…writing letters, etcetera. I had many connections with Mohun Bagan. This was important. But you must speak to Ronnie. And you must speak to Gordon Jones. He was the team manager. He invited a number of his friends to play on the tour. He was a good man."

"But what was your connection with Crook Town?"

"Ah...I was the club doctor. Of course, many of the players were my patients anyway as a general practitioner. But I was also the doctor for the club....You would like a cup of tea? My wife will fetch you one and I will tell you what you need to know."

Before they met

Crook, November 1920

So, the twenties were all about the great jazz age? The decadent world of The Great Gatsby and swingin' at The Hot Club are the enduring images of the time. Scandalous new fashions and marathon dances incurred the disapproval of the older generation – now there's a surprise. The innovative sounds of Duke Ellington and Jelly Roll Morton spread the new musical gospel from New Orleans and Chicago to the rest of a Western World populated by wildly enthusiastic youngsters eager to put the straight jacket of post-war austerity behind them. This was a time to shed those inhibitions and have a good time.

In 1920 the men recently returned from the bloodbath of the Great War could barely contain their excitement as they 'flapped' their way into the ranks of the million unemployed in Britain. Across the pond, the isolationist Warren Harding became president and gangs began to rule the streets as a national act to establish prohibition was passed. Not much chance of a drink there, then. Black folk gaily danced the Charleston in appreciation of the white supremacists joining the growing ranks of the Ku Klux Klan in the southern states. Miners, unable to prevent their feet from tapping out a crazy rhythm to the new tunes, were driven to delirious levels of happiness as they withheld their labour for an extra two shillings-a-week. Oh, how that jazz age put a smile on every face.

In Crook, Co. Durham, baby Ronald James was heaved into the world on the 8th of November. It was a world where he, his two brothers and sister had to wash in the pantry if they wanted any privacy. There was no sanitation to speak of and no indoor facilities. This was a coal mining town of back to back terraces where life was hard and football was a blessed relief. Set in a valley, Crook would often be viewed from the surrounding hills as nothing more than a thick, lifeless blanket of smog. This was life for real people in 1920. The Great Gatsby my arse!

But it wasn't unremitting misery for Ron growing up in Crook. The mines had brought a degree of prosperity to the town – this is all relative you understand. Trade was brisk, living conditions were improving and those lynchpins of the community, the church, miners' welfare, pubs and market were thriving. Saturday was market day and the buying and selling would go on until nine or ten at night with acetylene and pressure lamps hissing and sizzling above the stalls to draw in the custom. Poultry, ironmongery, fish, fruit, clothes and shoes could all be purchased. Or if you fancied a decent young pig it would set you back around ten shillings. Ready-for-the-pot rabbits – with a free onion thrown in – and mouthwatering homemade sweets, set the taste buds dancing. All this and fish and chips from a horse drawn wagon made the vitality of market day a focus of life in Crook.

The other great touchstone for the community was their football team. Crook Town, playing out of the Millfield ground, was established as one of the top amateur teams in the north eventually amassing five Northern League championships and famously, winning the FA Amateur Cup on five occasions including four visits to Wembley between 1954 and 1964. However, in the 1920-21 season, Ronnie James' first as a fully formed and functioning human being, the club would take a trip to a more distant destination. They took a short break at the end of March to play four games against a rapidly developing Spanish team called Barcelona who just happened to be managed by an Englishman. In fact, Jack Greenwell was not only English he was also a son of Crook and an ex Millfield player. So, you all thought that Terry Venables was the first Englishman to make buttock imprints on the Barca managerial chair? Well, now you know. He was just a pale imitation of the original, a miner's boy from Crook. Although, another local boy, Bobby Robson, also filled the seat a few years later. The team ran onto the Compo De La Industria field before four capacity crowds of 15,000 losing three times and drawing once. Barcelona later moved to the purpose built Nou Camp when they realised that old Compo was getting a bit uncomfortable.

The question is; how does a team like Crook become best footballing buddies with a club like Barcelona? The answer is Jack Greenwell. He had been an outstanding wing-half for his home town team before transferring to West Auckland in 1909. They then famously travelled to Italy to win the Sir Thomas Lipton Trophy – the unofficial first 'World Cup'. They repeated the feat in 1911 by which time Jack had returned to Crook. However, his European contact had been made. He married a Spanish lass and emigrated to the Iberian Peninsular where he signed for an emerging young team called Barcelona. The players and officials at Crook were grateful for this Catalonian contact and on 17th April 1913, embarked on a first trip to the land of the rising salary. On this first tour, Crook Town won one and drew three games with players such as the allegedly 'big and raw boned' Frank Smith, a description you can't quite imagine being applied to one of his sophisticated Latino opponents. They also witnessed first hand and to their great amusement the sight of an injured player being replaced by another, fitter version. What a hoot! Fifty-two years later, English football grasped the concept and introduced substitutes into the game. It had been hoped that the Spanish king, Alphonso, might attend some of the games but he declined after a recent attempt on his life made him a bit jumpy about public appearances. Nevertheless, Crook established their penchant for foreign travel and their old boy, Jack Greenwell established his credentials as a top British football export going on to manage Barca, the Spanish national team and following a sharp exit when the Civil War started, spells in Turkey and South America, managing Peru. He died in Santa Fe in 1945 aged sixty-one.

As Jack Greenwell's Barcelona and Crook Town continued their unlikely affair in 1921 - a bit like Sophia Loren having a fling with Jimmy Nail - Burnley were pressing on to the first division championship at a time when only three divisions existed. Tottenham were on a run that would see them pip Wolverhampton Wanderers to lift the FA Cup in the final at Stamford Bridge and the great Herbert Chapman joined Huddersfield as manager. He would go to win three consecutive championships with the Town team and become the dominant figure of this football era.

Meanwhile, in India, football was still dominated by the British who had introduced the game and formed the first Asian football league, the Calcutta League, in 1898. A rapidly developing football team called Mohun Bagan, part of the multi-sport Mohun Bagan Athletic Club, was challenging the all-conquering Calcutta FC and the assorted British army teams that competed in the league. They would finish as runners-up in 1920 and 1921 but had to wait until 1939 before celebrating their first championship on the fiftieth anniversary of their formation. In the year that war engulfed the world, Crook Town finished bottom of the Northern League on the fiftieth anniversary of *their* formation.

It seems that the gods had decreed that mother football would give birth to twins in 1889 when Crook Town and Mohun Bagan entered the world at exactly the same time. Unfortunately, while baby Crook remained at home and was raised in the school of hard knocks, baby Mohun was adopted by the Indian middle classes and enjoyed a rather more privileged upbringing. Like many siblings, their lives and fortunes have diverged but they eventually got back in touch.

Young Ronnie James was oblivious to such exotic distractions as the Indian sub-continent following the tried and tested route of his father and forefathers into the grim reality of the County Durham coal mines. It was what you did if you came from Crook. We met at Ronnie's home of fifty-two years in a council house on a hill overlooking Millfield where his team played and he was a life long fan. He had moved into the house with his wife of four years, Jenny, in 1951. The new homes were a revelation with electricity and indoor facilities. A bathroom and even a small garden added to the feeling that the hard work was finally being rewarded and ordinary people were able to live in more dignified surroundings. What we now regard as the most basic of conditions was regarded then as a huge advance. Ronnie and Jenny thought it a palace.

I was greeted at the Acacia Gardens front door by a tall, slim but stooping figure in slippers and an old track suit bottom. The kids were cycling up and down the hill in warm March sunshine careful to avoid the same broken glass I had circumnavigated to park the car. The view from the house was of more red brick houses, just like this one where other men just like Ronnie had moved their families to escape the primitive conditions of old Crook.

"Hello. I wondered if you were coming or not."

"You must be Ronnie. I'm Steven Chaytor. Sorry I'm a bit late. Crook's easy enough to find but Acacia gardens was a bit of a stretch."

I'm beckoned through into the back room where a smokeless fuel fire is glowing brightly behind one of those glass-fronted fire doors that seemed to be all the rage in the seventies. The flames flickered silently behind the glass strips ensuring a ready supply of domestic hot water and a sleepy, warmth that immediately caused my eyelids to relax. If I'd so wished, I could have fallen asleep in seconds. Ronnie's chair was by the fire. He dispensed with the dinner party niceties and pointless preamble and went straight to the purpose of our meeting. Rather like a couple of gangsters doing a bit of business, I thought. "All right. We both know why we're here. The money's in the case. No need to count it. It's all there. Now, you've got what you want. I don't expect to see you again. When you leave…don't look back." But Ronnie had his slippers on, so I knew he wasn't a gangster.

"I dug out this book and some paper clippings. It's all I've got now. I gave the rest away for safe keeping. I wanted to be sure it was all kept together when I'm gone. Michael's got it….There….sit down."

Ronnie's voice was quiet, monotone...sad. He rarely looked up from the floor. Jenny had died in January 1998 after fifty years together. His son had been killed in a road accident in 1966. He was estranged from his daughter. Pneumoconiosis, the miners' disease of the lungs, vibration white finger, the miners' circulation disease and a range of other age-related ailments had ravaged the body of my host.

" I don't get out any more. I can't."

Ronnie had worked in the Roddymoor pit from 1937 to 1953 when it closed and he transferred to the Hole-in the-Wall pit, nearby. Redundancy came in 1964 with another closure. There was no pay out and no pension. He worked in the stores department of an engineering firm, ATM, until 1980 when he retired. At least there was a small pension with the last job. He and Jenny loved to dance though. And dance they did. They also loved Crook Town and followed the team with a passion. Jenny James, Drybrough's Northern League supporter of the year, 1984. The newspaper cuttings and the coveted award a testimony to just how passionate and dedicated they were. As the football talk usurped the conversation, so the eyes raised and brightened, the voice became animated and the face betrayed a pleasure that only good memories can bring.

"Here...look at this. I've never shown anyone this before."

Now, normally, if a man in his slippers relaxing in the drowsy warmth of the afternoon made such a suggestion, I'd be worried about hearing the duelling banjos in the background. On this occasion I could discern that the intentions were pure and innocent, though I wasn't quite sure what to expect as Ronnie heaved himself forward to stretch his arms towards his feet. As he wrenched backward he pulled up a trouser leg to reveal a lower limb that appeared little more than a bone.

"I shattered that in an accident when I was seven....look at it....
They reckoned I wouldn't be able to do owt with it." He laughed at
his own limb.

"Could you play then? You know, what with the leg and everything?"

"Oh, aye. Left back. I used to shove books inside my socks to make
it look thicker and so people wouldn't look at it. I played for Jobs
Hill Home Guard during the war and was picked for Durham County

fire service against Northumberland in 1943. I was a part-time fireman as well. Northumberland were all ex-pros. We got stuffed 1-0. A bloke who played outside-right for Wolves in 1939 was playing for them....can't remember his name. He tried to get me to sign for Wolves after the war. Anyway, I couldn't get away from the pit. The chance was gone."

"So what about the India trip, Ronnie? How come you were involved?"

"Oh, aye. The India trip. You know, the most important time in Crook's history was in 1931. I remember it. I was only ten or eleven. They were trying to buy the ground so when we drew Leicester City in the FA Cup, the committee decided to switch the tie to Filbert Street to get more money from the gate receipts. Why, the fans weren't best pleased. Some of them had never been further than Bishop Auckland. They couldn't afford to go to Leicester. A lot of them boycotted the club. It took a long time to recover from that."

"So, how come you were involved with India?"

"They used to get thousands there in those days, you know...Aye, we had a good team then.....Oh, aye.....India. You want to talk about India. Well, I was the assistant secretary of the club in 1975."

Calcutta, July 1934

1934 was a pivotal year in the history of Europe. As the German President, Field-Marshall Paul von Hindenburg lay dying in Neudeck, Hitler's cabinet enacted a law combining the offices of Chancellor and President into one. Thus, on the old boy's death on August 2nd, Adolf Hitler became Fuhrer of the Third Reich and effective dictator of Germany.

Meanwhile in Spain, the fledgling republic was beset by regional and industrial unrest with widespread bloodshed and military intervention. In Barcelona, an Independent Catalan Republic was proclaimed but this too was put down by the police and the military. Further north in Marseilles, the King of Yugoslavia, Alexander 1, was assassinated whilst on a state visit to France. Driving through the Place de la Bourse with the French Foreign Minister, Louis Barthou, he was gunned down by a shabbily dressed loner who had burst through the police cordon and jumped onto the running board of the royal car. The gunman was cut down by a sabre wielding, mounted soldier before being savagely beaten and left for dead by the irate crowd.

On April 29th, the Italian parliament gave Mussolini dictatorial powers, which he promptly used on June 23rd when he decided to invade Albania. And in Austria a socialist revolt had been brutally crushed on the 17th February.

All in all, 1934 was not a good year for choosing a holiday from the Key Camp brochure.

For those deciding on their vacation location it was probably best to avoid Europe. Or was it? Perhaps a walking holiday in China would appeal. Why not join the Red Army of Mao Tse-tung as they set out on 'The Long March' of October 16th? Then again, maybe an adventure holiday for couples sounded attractive. You could have joined couriers Bonnie and Clyde in Louisiana USA had they not died in a hail of bullets in May after their four-year bank-robbing safari.

Thankfully, as the world order was breaking down and heading for another monumental, global conflict, there was some good news. Hollywood heart-throb Gary Cooper was making 'The lives of a Bengal Lancer' and that other throbber of hearts, Ronald Coleman was starring in 'Clive of India'.

Truly, through the lens of a movie camera, the sun would never set on the British Empire. This illusion of empirical permanence was even maintained in India itself as Gandhi suspended the campaign of civil disobedience on April 7th.

The combination of events in Hollywood and India were actually a beautifully orchestrated manoeuvre designed to prepare the world for the birth of the man who would eventually lead Crook Town to the banks of the Hooghly. It would become the first and only football team to visit Calcutta and play in one of the world's most famous cricket arenas. On the 1st July 1934, Arun Banerjee was born. Father was a well-heeled businessman and mother was, well, a full time mother. Who wouldn't be with ten children? He was born into the Brahmin caste, the highest of the Hindu religion and was surrounded not only by a huge family but the servants and household that accompanied his place in society. It was also in 1934 that the Eden Gardens cricket ground was itself born as a test match arena. Fittingly, the inaugural test was against England, the country that had effectively created the modern Calcutta.

The Banerjee family was well known in Calcutta, not only in society and business but also in sporting circles. Arun's father, Haradahan, was a top amateur footballer in a country where non-professional teams were still regarded as the pinnacle of the game. He was a member of the Mohun Bagan Athletic Club that hosted, amongst other things, football, cricket, athletics and hockey. Indeed, he was a free-scoring centre forward for Bagan from 1933-39 and was selected to represent India on a tour of New Zealand in this, the year of Arun Banerjee's birth. Unfortunately he was unable to travel due to a family commitment but his original selection underlined his quality. Mohun Bagan, even then regarded as one of the country's top teams and later to be known as the 'Manchester United of India', played regularly to sell-out crowds of 35,000 polite and well-behaved spectators against local rivals Calcutta FC and East Bengal, with whom Mohun Bagan shared a stadium. At the beginning of each season the Athletic Club would re-open their club tent that would serve as the clubhouse, and changing facilities for the football team. This was a tradition in Indian sport that developed technically in order to preserve open space and was a major social occasion for club members. However, we are not talking about a tent in the manner you and I would understand. This was essentially a solid construction with the only difference being the canvas roof, which would in fact look like a ridge tent. Legally, the tent would be vacated for at least a month at the end of each season to confirm its 'temporary' status. Mind you, the Manchester United of India didn't have Mancunian weather to contend with. It's not difficult to imagine the consequences of erecting a tent at Old Trafford.

The family sporting tradition was also followed by Arun's uncles, one of whom, Dr. Alarihor Banerjee, became the Indian breast stroke champion and was also selected for rifle shooting at the 1948 London Olympics. Unfortunately, a family illness and pressure of work were to prevent him from becoming an Olympian in London. But his expertise at rifle shooting would be recognised with victory at the Bisley Rifle Shooting Championships in 1950 and appearances at the next three Olympic Games at Helsinki, Melbourne and Rome. To complete the sporting set, another uncle succeeded in becoming the Indian table tennis champion.

Back in England, Herbert Chapman, manager of the all-conquering, three-titles-in-a-row Arsenal team, was mourned by the football world after his sudden death in January 1934. Meanwhile, Manchester United languished in the second division wishing they were the Mohun Bagan of England instead of a yo-yo team unable to challenge the heavyweights of Sunderland, Everton, Huddersfield, Manchester City and of course, Arsenal. Manchester City compounded the United misery by beating Portsmouth 2-1 to win the FA Cup at Wembley. Stan Matthews, Alex James, Matt Busby, Cliff Bastin and 'Dixie' Dean were the stars of a time before television, before the war, before advertising on shirts and before David Beckham's dad was born. But it was Arsenal that dominated throughout the thirties winning five Championships, two FA Cups and five Charity Shields in the days when there was nothing else to win. Herbert Chapman had fashioned a team that was described as 'horribly mean in defence and cruel in counter-attack'. Their football was known as 'smash and grab' and led to the epithet, 'Lucky Arsenal' – which, of course, they have been for the past seventy years.

On the world football scene, Italy were embarking on a period of domination as they took the world cup, beating Czechoslovakia (whatever happened to them) 2-1 in Rome before 50,000 fans. They were presented with the trophy by a strutting Mussolini who went on to form a devastating partnership up front for Fascist United with twin striker, Hitler. Italy went on to retain the Jules Rimet Trophy in 1938 with a 4-2 win over Hungary in Paris. These were the days when England didn't bother with such vulgar distractions as world cups, content in the sure knowledge that we had invented the game so if anyone wanted to play us, they could bloody well come to England.

Growing up in the cosmopolitan chaos of nineteen thirties Calcutta was a delight for the young Arun Banerjee. Educated in the fee paying, private school system that was the staple for those of his caste gave Arun the start in life that his mother, in particular, craved. She had always wanted her son to become a doctor and the bright, sport loving boy didn't disappoint. He was presented with his Brahmin Thread aged thirteen, qualified for the University of Calcutta at the age of fifteen and went on to study medicine at the RG Kar Medical College, competing for Mohun Bagan at football as a student. His mother couldn't have written a better script. The club encouraged student membership and had the strictest standards of discipline designed to develop the mind and the body. Members would be expelled for smoking and coaches would even stop the young sportsmen in their tracks to test them on academic matters. As you read these words I imagine you are picturing the grinning court jester that was the boy Gascoigne being interrupted during a thirty-minute shuttle run session to test him on his two-times table. Thankfully, there's more than one way to produce a decent footballer.

As a Hindu Brahmin, Arun had 'a start' in Indian society and life for him in the capital city of West Bengal was "quite wonderful". Calcutta is often viewed as a heaving, seething mass of humanity. At once, ugly and desperate yet colourful and exciting. It is regarded as the cultural capital of India and was once known as the capital of British India since it was a largely the creation of British traders and merchants. But Arun would see the last of the best years before partition from muslim East Bengal and the eventual creation of the state of Bangladesh that caused a flood of refugees to the city. Coupled with a post war population explosion this caused Calcutta to become something of an urban horror story. At least in 1934 it was relatively simple to get around the city. The man-powered rickshaw ruled. Nowadays, the city is choked with cars, fumes and over fourteen million people, so it's not the place to go for a quiet weekend.

The young Dr. Banerjee practised medicine in his home city, at one stage holding the position of medical officer to the Indian railways. However, when presented with the opportunity to take a position in England, specialising in geriatrics at Hartlepool General Hospital, the prospect proved too exciting to refuse. He had been married only eighteen months earlier to Jayasree but it was a great career move and a chance to expand their experience of the world. So it was that in the closing weeks of 1966, Arun and Jayasree Banerjee arrived at Heathrow airport and England became their home.

Between 1966 and 1972 the Banerjees moved around with the doctor's various jobs in Walsall, Sunderland, Rotherham, Newcastle and Cleethorpes before the opportunity of a general practise became available in Crook, County Durham. The football mad medic was soon enlisted as the club doctor for local team, Crook Town and he threw himself wholeheartedly into the role, lending support to the club as a fan as well as medical officer. The family thought about returning home to India on a number of occasions but war with Pakistan and the birth of their children gradually convinced them that Crook was home.

Sedgefield, March 1943

If you're a film star and you've got a cleavage like that belonging to Jane Russell, then you'd better make the most of it. That was the one thought in the mind of millionaire nutcase, movie dilettante and aircraft engineer, Howard Hughes as he assumed the role of producer-director of the controversial western, The Outlaw. Hughes had recently fired the original director, Howard Hawkes, from the ailing project.

"We're not getting enough production from Jane's breasts."

The designer of the monster aircraft, 'The Spruce Goose' then set about engineering a brassiere to enhance the actress's most famous features. He did such a good job that the double-barrelled shotgun rendered the picture too racy for the Joseph Breen Production Code Administration and it only received a token release in San Francisco in February 1943. Naturally, Russell went on to be a 'big' star and Hughes decided to grow his finger nails and live as a self-imposed, sanitised recluse.

As the war raged around the globe, Hollywood also unleashed upon an unsuspecting public, 'The Song of Bernadette'. The hitherto unknown Jennifer Jones played a sickly French peasant girl who has a vision of The Virgin Mary in a grotto by a rubbish dump. In a blink of an eye she turned Lourdes, an equally unknown and unassuming French town, into the pilgrimage capital of France – and an interesting and novel commercial opportunity to boot.

In the world of football, the English leagues had been suspended since the outbreak of war in September 1939. Hundreds of playing careers were interrupted, many lost their peak years to the war, some never returned. There were local fixtures in which many top professionals turned out for the club that was nearest to where they were stationed for national service and there were war-time internationals to maintain the football spirits and keep the sporting juices flowing.

In India, there was no such suspension as Mohun Bagan won their second Calcutta League championship losing just one match in a season of dominance and supported enthusiastically by a nine-year-old Hindu boy called Arun Banerjee. He had returned to the city with his family the previous year after being evacuated to their holiday home north of Calcutta in 1941. Having believed it was safe to return to their home, he had to watch in horror as the Japanese bombed their home city. An increasingly chaotic, commercial metropolis began to slide into economic decline as the war took its toll and the prospect of partition grew ever more likely. In sharp contrast, the Hindu dominated Mohun Bagan was becoming ever more successful in both the league and the IFA Shield, the Indian equivalent of the FA Cup. Rivals, the East Bengal Club, who shared the same ground, continued to share dominance of domestic competitions with the muslim only Mohamedan Sporting Club pitching in as the third of the 'big three'. Football was becoming a major spectator attraction and radio was beginning to take an enthusiastic interest in the sport. Matches between the rivals would eventually be accompanied by live coverage, which would have whole streets glued to the wireless sets and households supporting the rival teams turning up the volume and cheering as if actually present at the game. This would turn into a kind of decibel contest on the Calcutta streets as opposing supporters sought to beat each other back with noise.

Back in England, on the 6th of March 1943, a week after the RAF bombed Berlin in daylight for the first time, Gordon Jones became his parents little miracle when he was squeezed into the world. His world was Sedgefield in Co. Durham, a village that would become known for a racecourse, a prime minister and a strange, ritualistic, Shrove Tuesday ball game involving hundreds of players and no rules. This brand of mayhem is believed to have provided the origins of the very game that Gordon would go on to grace as a professional player. In an interesting tweak of the fates, he actually lived for some time in the house that is now 'Ministers' restaurant, so called because of the Sedgefield connection to two prime ministers, local MP Tony Blair and Anthony Eden, who lived just outside of the village for a while. Only a Liberal prime minister is required for Sedgefield to get the full set – Hmm.

In the early days it was not necessarily the famous professionals that inspired the boy Jones. He was educated at the Rectory Row school in the village and as a youngster his football heroes were the men who played in the local leagues. Local football had a quality then that is perhaps lacking now since the maximum wage structure had the effect of keeping more talent in the amateur arena where a working man could also earn some decent 'boot money'. The players were accessible and real and the football was hard and exciting. Gordon Jones wanted to play football. By the age of fifteen, he was on the ground staff at Middlesbrough FC and made his debut for them in The League Cup, aged sixteen. So, Gordon Jones did play football. In fact, he played rather a lot of football, going on to make a post-war record 528 league appearances for 'The Boro' and receiving nine caps for England at under twenty three level. Unfortunately, the full England cap eluded him when injury struck at the wrong time and he missed out on the 1966 world cup squad, for which he was widely tipped.

Rather than being fitted for the World Cup squad suit, Gordon was forced to sit out the finals like most of the population of Britain and watch Bobby Charlton score that amazing goal in the 2-0 victory over Mexico. Gathering the ball on the half way line, he surged forward, dropping his shoulder to wrong foot two defenders before unleashing a right foot shot that near broke the net. Out on the right wing was a man with a rather closer view of the action. This would be the only World Cup appearance of Southampton star, Terry Paine. More of whom late.

For Gordon Jones, this was as close as he would get to the big break that he so desired. Nevertheless, he continued with Middlesbrough for another six years before taking the short journey to Darlington to close out his professional career at Feethams. And so it was that he found himself out of contract in the summer 1975. Aged thirty-two he was forced to confront the reality that every footballer faces at some time, the end of his playing days. What to do next? He had business interests outside the game, so as much as he loved it, he wasn't dependent on football for a living. After declining a number of offers to get back into the game in various capacities, he received a phone call from a representative from Northern League Crook Town. His long and distinguished career appeared well past its autumn years but little did he know, it was heading for an unexpected Indian summer.

Argentina, July 1978

It's the second phase of the eleventh World Cup and South America has Poland surrounded as Peru, Brazil and the host nation, Argentina are grouped together with the European outsiders. Peru lose their first match 0-3 to Brazil and Poland 0-2 to the 'The Argies'. We are not happy. Inevitably, Brazil and Argentina draw 0-0 to ensure that the group will be decided by the final pair of matches. In the encounter between the seeming no-hopers, Peru and Poland, the Poles snatch a 1-0 victory to give themselves an outside hope of an unlikely appearance in the World Cup final. However, the game will be remembered, not for the Polish victory but for the inexplicable actions of the Peru goalkeeper, Quiroga, a man known around the football world as 'El Loco' because of his crazy dashes into enemy territory for no apparent reason. As if suddenly possessed by the spirit of some ancient Peruvian postman, he would take flight from his goal and gallop the length of the pitch and back seemingly chased by the spirit of an ancient Peruvian dog. On this occasion, he chose to brutally hack down a bemused opponent who had the temerity to attempt to exploit his absence from the goal. Presumably, he could have claimed that the player had been possessed by the spirit of the ancient Peruvian dog and he had acted to defend himself from an inevitable mauling. However, as if snapped back to reality by the shrill whistle of the gods, he draws away from the incident, hands clasped behind his back and staring with incredulity at the man in black, who is clearly a referee and not a clergyman come to exorcise the evil spirit. El Loco appears totally unaware of what he has just done and why he is in the centre circle. Tough shit. This is a football match. The referee books him, he returns to his goalmouth, the crowd can scarcely believe what they've seen and we sit at home peeing ourselves. The man in black is Pat Partridge, England's premier official and a man who, two years previously, had refereed every match in the Crook Town tour of India.

Oh....in the final group matches, Brazil beat Poland 3-1 then Argentina pulverised Peru 6-0 to win through on goal difference. El Loco was forced into print to defend the integrity of his team-mates against claims of bribery and match fixing. Quiroga was born in Argentina, by the way.

!978 was not a good year to be a pope. The Catholic Church was going through them like they'd gone out of fashion. Someone had installed a revolving door in The Vatican and if you possessed a tall hat and a long coat, you were in with a shout. Three in one year, including Cardinal Albino Luciani who lasted just thirty-three days as Pope John Paul 1, the shortest tenure since 1605. There was a great deal of speculation about the cause of his death. Was it a plot? Was he 'eliminated'? Personally, I was a bit concerned about his surname. His successor, Cardinal Karol Wojtyla must have had a few doubts when he took over on October 16th but he needn't have worried. He's still going strong in 2003.

All this talk of popes and religion reminds me that 1978 was a very good year for rock music with the Ausie head-bangers, AC/DC chalking up their first UK hit record, " Rock 'N' Roll Damnation", followed by the equally choir-busting "Highway To Hell". Does The Devil have all the good music? They're still going strong in 2003.

Twenty-five years on, Pat Partridge is also still going strong. We meet, on a warm, almost sultry May evening, at his hilltop farm home near Bishop Auckland where two picture windows in the lounge reveal views of County Durham and the Dales that have to be seen to be believed. I have no doubt that many of the good folk from the south of England are still completely unaware that Co. Durham can widen and brighten the eyes in such a way.

"When I'm too old to get upstairs, I want my bed putting down here so all I'll need to do is lift my head ...then I'll be able to see all that. They'll take me out of here in a box."

The early moments of our conversation have a truly surreal air. After establishing that he's playing golf next Wednesday at Carlisle he reveals that he's expecting a call any time now from Brian Johnson, no less than the lead singer with AC/DC. Take a minute to assimilate that piece of information and ask yourself if you might have imagined two more unlikely golf partners. One of the world's most respected referees, a profession of correctness, propriety and not much pay and one of the world's leading rock singers, an anti-establishment profession of anarchy, rebellion and large wads of cash. There... you see... people from all walks of life and all corners of the world brought together by eighteen holes, fourteen clubs a Pringle sweater and a pair of slacks. Geordie, Brian is flying in from the US and presumably wants a lift to Carlisle to appear on the next leg of the northern celebrity charity golf circuit. Brendan Healy, Tim Healy and John Miles amongst others are part of the gang.

"You should see the cabaret after the meal. John Miles can make a

guitar sing."

"So, does Brian Johnson still wear the old cloth cap, then?"

"Oh, yeh. All that curly, grey hair sticking out from underneath. A great bloke. Turned up in his Bentley last time."

For those of you unfamiliar with the strains of AC/DC, Brian Johnson is not exactly Aled Jones. His is a classic rock voice akin to a chain saw or a Ford Cortina without a silencer or an angry lion with a touch of helium. His voice wouldn't just shatter a champagne glass, it would obliterate the bottle and vaporise the contents. Imagining him shouting "Fore" after a misdirected shot is unnerving to say the least. But they say that Alice Cooper is a bit nifty from tee to green so perhaps golf is the new rock 'n' roll.

Pat revels in his renewed celebrity with an almost child-like glee, modestly comparing himself with the world famous multi-millionaires he mixes with on the charity golf circuit. But lest we forget, he was at the very top of his (albeit amateur) profession for several years. From his first league match, Barrow versus Stockport County, in 1965 to his last, Nottingham Forest versus Coventry on 2nd May 1981, he established a reputation second to none with a whistle and a pencil. On his final international assignment, Austria versus Bulgaria, the whole Bulgarian team signed and presented a match ball to him. To top it all, the great Austrian striker Hanz Krankl approached Pat after the game and made a personal gesture as a mark of his respect.

"Mr. Patrick...here is my shirt."

He refereed his first match in 1953 at the age of nineteen when he officiated for his works team, Head Wrightson versus Crosswaites. His first class ticket was achieved in 1957, his league debut in 1965 and his ascendancy to the FIFA list in 1971. The FA Cup final of 1975 and World Cup of 1978 followed, leading to eventual retirement aged forty-eight in 1982. Twenty-nine years a referee and every single game recorded in small hard back note books. You can ask Pat Partridge who and where he was officiating at any given time and he'll take about ten seconds to give you an accurate answer and recall some deeply obscure detail to boot. These are historic documents.

"So how did you get involved with the India tour?"

"I had nothing to do with Crook Town. They just asked me if I would go to referee the tour matches. Apparently the Indians asked if Crook could get the 1975 Cup final ref. Well it was easy for them 'cos I lived on the doorstep. I thought 'well, if I can get Margaret along, it'll be a bit of a holiday as well'."

"So you said yes?"

"I cleared it with the FA and that was that. Actually, I mention it in my autobiography. 'Oh Ref!' – a play on 'Oh Calcutta'. Get it? It was doing the rounds at the time. Have you read it?"

"Ah, well.....er no. I must have missed it. I'll have to get a copy."

Wembley, July 1966

The world in 1958 was just emerging from the post war period of austerity and reflection. It was entering a phase of renewal and revival with a growing optimism and a sense of the burgeoning role and identity of youth in society. Teenagers were born in the fifties. But in a stark reminder of the reality of a post war world, Elvis Presley, the greatest youth icon of them all, was drafted into the US army. The United States was still a place where Martin Luther King could be arrested for loitering in Alabama and mindful of one of the last acts of the war, the Campaign for Nuclear Disarmament was formed in Great Britain.

English football was dominated by Wolverhampton Wanderers, who won the League Championship and Bolton Wandereers, who won the FA Cup. The World Cup would be hosted by Sweden and England, who had decided to join the party in 1950, would take part in the competition but with a tragically depleted squad. Having said that football was dominated by Wolves and Bolton, that was only with regard to results. In truth, the football world was dominated by an event that would define a club, create a legend and alter the course of sporting history.

At approximately 3.05pm on the 6th February 1958 a twenty-year-old footballer lay motionless and unconscious in a pool of melted snow. The skies were dark, snow flurries whipped around the air and orange flames leaped from a mangled wreck but a few yards away. He was still strapped into the aircraft seat he had been clinging to as the BEA Elizabethan airliner struggled to take off from Munich airport under darkened skies and in blizzard conditions. Unknown to him, he had been thrown from the stricken craft when it had split asunder following a catastrophic failure to gain height. After failing to clear a fence, crossing a road, then hitting a house with the port wing, the starboard side of the fuselage careered into a wooden hut and the cockpit smashed into a tree. The aeroplane had been carrying Britain's most famous football team, Manchester United, on their way home from a European Cup tie in Belgrade. The famous 'Busby Babes' were on board. Seven had been killed. Roger Byrne, Tommy Taylor, Mark Jones, Eddie Coleman, Billy Whelan, David Pegg and Geoff Bent were the immediate, tragic victims. Duncan Edwards, destined to be an all time great, died a few days later in hospital.

The motionless player in the melted snow was Bobby Charlton. Beside him was an equally lifeless Dennis Violet. Fearing the broken craft was about to explode, goalkeeper, Harry Gregg, who had been running back and forth from the wreckage to help recover survivors, grabbed both of the bodies by the belt and heaved them to a safe distance. A safe distance, but they may heave been dead already. Gregg, heroically, returned again and again to the burning debris to assist Matt Busby and then Jackie Blanchflower. When he turned to head back to Bobby and Dennis, he was stunned to find them both standing staring into the fire, shocked, silent and bewildered. They had survived. The Munich air disaster was the death of twenty-three people including eight of the world's finest footballers. It was also the day that the Bobby Charlton the world came to know was born.

Two things happened to Bobby Charlton following the tragedy that created a legend. Firstly, he became an instant regular in the United team where previously he had been gradually working his way to prominence with a remarkable set of peers. He was now a senior squad member ahead of his time and with responsibilities beyond his years. Secondly, it is widely believed that the disaster changed his personality. Once happy, joking and innocent he was now deeply affected by his escape from death. Guilt at surviving when others hadn't? Scarred by the loss of his friends and colleagues? Whatever the combination of factors, it affected Bobby to such an extent that thirty-two years later in a 1990 interview with Eamon Dunphy for his book on Matt Busby, Charlton was moved to tears at the very thought of the crash. In a 2001 interview with Hunter Davies for the BBC, he revealed that he thought about the crash every single day. The events of Munich would shape the player and the man.

Through the rest of his playing career and beyond he was regarded as bright, intelligent and sensitive but not for his joyous approach to life. He may have been regarded as somewhat reticent, even surly, certainly private but Bobby Charlton was at the centre of some of the pivotal moments of modern British football history. First there was the Munich air crash. Then there was the legendary rebuilding of Manchester United. There was the first English European Cup victory in 1968, the memorable Brazil encounter in 1970 and the ill-fated substitution of Bobby against West Germany in the same competition. There was a, then record, 106 England caps and still a record, 49 international goals. But most of all and best of all there was 1966.

Bobby Charlton will forever be remembered as one of the eleven players who took on West Germany at Wembley on Saturday July 30th, and won. The World Cup came to England for the first and only time. It would eventually lead to a knighthood for Bobby and immortality in the football world. The game would be seen and heard all over the world, including India, where Bobby Charlton would become the most famous world player and a symbol of all that was best about English football. In Calcutta, Dr. Arun Banerjee heard the match crouched around a radio along with the vast majority of the Indian nation. Televisions were a rarity back then. Back in England, the whole nation watched as our heroes triumphed. Gordon Jones, resigned to not making the England squad watched from the comfort of home in Fairfield, Stockton on Tees. Ronnie James viewed proceedings with his wife and daughter at home in Crook and Pat Partridge cheered on his compatriots and no doubt had a view on the Russian linesman from home in Acklam, Middlesbrough. Although he did get closer to the action when as a new League list referee, he was invited by top official, Jim Finney, to meet the match officials operating at Ayresome Park, one of the World cup venues. Meanwhile, Terry Paine had a fantastic view but had to bear the disappointment of sitting on the England bench as one of the eleven squad members who weren't selected that day.

Bobby's 1966 heroics were also rewarded by the Football Writers with their Player of the Year award and the title European Footballer of the Year. This was a man at the top of his profession, admired throughout the world and now guaranteed a place in history. And even though, by the time of the Crook tour in 1976, he had retired from League football after an unsuccessful stint as player-manager at Preston North end, he was still 'The Great Bobby Charlton', England's finest.

INDIA WELCOMES CROOK TOWN FC

It Was Just
A Thought

Millfield, August 1975

If a picture paints a thousand ships, then why can't I paint you? If Telly Savalas could sing a note, then my name's Fanny Craddock. If the great British public could take that song to number two in the hit parade (alright, the charts), then why weren't we all taken away for electric shock treatment? Book him Danno.

If Britain could embrace the 'art' – for that is what it is – of streaking, such as the famous incident in the Lords test match when one such 'artiste' nearly whipped off the bails with his exuberance, then why couldn't we have a female leader of the conservative party? If we could have a female leader of the conservative party, then why couldn't Charlie Chaplin get the knighthood he should have received years ago had it not been for his political views? Well, he bloody did, didn't he? And quite right too.

If the biggest film star of the year could be a giant shark with a nasty temper, a menacing theme tune and a set of teeth to die for, then why couldn't ex-government minister, John Profumo receive a CBE? After all, it was just reward for his central role in the eponymous affair of 1963 when he, Christine Keeler and Russian naval attache, Captain Ivanov played 'I spy with my little eye, something beginning with….S'.

"SECRET!"

"Oh, come on you naughty Captain….That's all you ever think about."

"SAUSAGE!"

"John, you're a cheeky boy. You've already had breakfast. I'll give you a clue….it's under the bed."

"SLIPPERS!"

"Well done boys. Two pairs in fact."

If Manchester United could win the second division championship a year after being relegated from the first by a back-heeled goal from one of their legendary former players, then why couldn't Jimmy Armfield lead Leeds United to the European Cup Final in Paris? Never mind that they were beaten 2-0 by Bayern Munich. Well, they did and he did. How fortunes change.

If Juan Carlos 1 was 'The Man Who Would be King', sworn in as the Spanish monarchy was re-established on the death of Generalissimo Francisco Franco, then why couldn't Sean Connery and Michael Caine appear in a classic film of the same name? The two, latter day celluloid knights of the realm starred in the film of the Rudyard Kipling story about two soldiers of fortune in India. In an interesting and novel twist, Connery employed a Scottish accent and Caine played a cockney.

If the FA Cup is the most romantic football competition in the world, then why couldn't second division Fulham win it against London rivals, West Ham? Unfortunately, they didn't, but in the Wembley final of 1975, romance did rear its head when Alan Taylor, a recent, unheralded purchase from Rochdale, scored the goals that took the Cup back to Upton Park. From Spotland obscurity to national acclaim and a cup-winner's medal in six months. The referee that day was Pat Partridge, one of England's top whistle blowers, a soon-to-be world cup official and a native of Cockfield, little more than an Ian Hutchinson long throw from Crook.

If Carlisle United could lead the First Division of the Football League after three matches of the 1974-75 season - now stop there and imagine that situation being replicated now. I know, it's absurd. Like suggesting Arvind Parmer will win Wimbledon or Iain Duncan Smith could become prime minister. Like backing Shergar to win next years Derby or Jeffrey Archer to win the Nobel Prize for Literature. These things simply will not happen. But back then, The Foxes from Brunton Park stunned the football world with one of the most unexpected rises in the history of the game. A fairy tale. Hans Christian Andersen must have been the manager. The centre half pairing must have been the Brothers Grimm – So what that they ended up being relegated. If all this could happen, then why couldn't unfashionable amateur teams travel to far off places on unlikely football tours?

If all these things could happen and a local boy could end up refereeing the FA Cup final, then why couldn't the players of Crook Town dream of travelling to India to appear against the most famous club in the old empire state? If they could dream about it, then why couldn't they do it?

It was a summer evening in August 1975 when members of the Crook Town committee had just finished a pre-season meeting and gathered for a

regular pint in the clubhouse bar with assorted drinking companions. If they'd had a juke box and if they'd switched it on, they could have tapped their feet to the number one sound of Typically Tropical with the truly gut-wrenchingly, toe-curlingly, mind-numbingly, teeth-grindingly, heart-sinkingly, awful "Oooo, We're Going To Barbados". Come back Telly Savalas. But something tells me that this would not have been to the taste of the assembled committee members. I have a sixth sense about such matters. Secretary, Richard Singleton, his assistant, Ronnie James, club doctor Arun Banerjee, chairman, Wilf Collingwood and treasurer, Herbert Hutchinson were all present as the football crack turned to India.

"You ever played football Doc? In India I mean?"

"Certainly. I was a sportsman. My father was a sportsman. I played for Mohun Bagan as a student."

"So who's that then? Never heard of them."

"They are India's most famous football team. Not well known in England, obviously. But the finest in all of India."

"Hey, that'd make a good tour. How about it, Dr. Banerjee? What do you reckon? We should go and play your old team. How about it, eh?"

The talk was whimsical and slightly teasing. But a little seed was sown onto a piece of fertile ground.

"Hmm. Why not. Maybe it could be arranged."

"Get away. You can't be serious. Us lot, tour India. Anyhow, we couldn't afford it."

"Why not? It should be possible. Anything is possible. I will make a call tomorrow."

"Aye, alright Doc.... Get them in. Mine's a pint"

The Search for a Star

Following the fateful meeting at Millfield in August 1975 it was down Dr. Banerjee to make the first move. He'd said it was possible. He'd said he could do it. He'd said he knew people. He was, after all, still a member of the Mohun Bagan Athletic Club, the most influential club in India. His father was still associated with the club. He was perfectly positioned to make the connection.

A quick telephone call to the family home in Calcutta was the first step. He asked his father a simple question,

"Do you think it is possible?"

The response was an equally simple answer,

"Yes. It should be possible."

Could it really be that easy?

It seems the Crook club was pushing at an open door. Mohun Bagan fell for the idea immediately. What the people at Crook hadn't realised was that serious football tours of India were a rarity since professional players were not allowed to take money out of the country so simply didn't come at all. In fact, this would be the first significant tour since the Second World War. Added to that was the high reputation that preceded Crook Town. They had not realised that their exploits as four times FA Amateur Cup Winners in the fifties and sixties had not gone unnoticed in a country becoming increasingly besotted by the round ball game. The Indian club's secretary, Dhiren Dey, was therefore immediately engaged in the task of compiling an itinerary to be suggested to the potential tourists. He became the chief organiser of the trip and warmed to his task with the enthusiasm of a company executive attempting to construct a raft from two bin liners and an old toilet seat in order to cross a lake on a management team building exercise. It was a challenge that could bring significant rewards and Shri Dey was able to deliver two options to an ever more excited Crook club who were actually beginning to believe the trip could happen.

The first option came via an invitation from the Indian Football Association (IFA) for a seven-day, all expenses paid tour that included an appearance in the IFA Shield, which was not restricted to Indian clubs. However, there were problems with the timing of the trip and the Football Association indicated that they would not sanction a tour that interfered with Crook's involvement in the FA Trophy. The approval of the FA was essential to the trip. The second offer came directly from Mohun Bagan and would involve playing five games in fourteen days with all expenses paid and the equivalent of £30 pocket money for each member of the touring party. Now that was an offer they couldn't refuse.

However, there was a slight catch. Dhiren Dey relayed the two conditions that Crook Town must meet in order that the tour could be promoted successfully in Calcutta. Firstly, the tour party should number twenty-one players and officials, one of whom should be a member of the 1966 World Cup winning squad. Secondly, the 1975 FA Cup Final referee should be invited to officiate at each game. They were keen to make an impact and were aiming high:

"Can you get Bobby Charlton?"

That was a tough one. We'll come to that later. However, the Mohun Bagan secretary had no idea that international referee and 1975 FA Cup Final official, Pat Partridge, lived just a few miles from the Millfield ground. Contacting him was simple. Pat loved the idea and after clearing his participation with the FA - and wife Margaret's inclusion on the trip - he signed up and completed one of the Indian conditions. One down, one to go.

In January 1976, Gordon Jones played his last game for Darlington and was released from the club. Temporarily out of football employment, he was approached by Crook Town to take the reins of the team following the departure of Don Heath. It was an interesting offer, he liked the people and it was made all the more appetising by the fact that the tour to India was still on the agenda. Had he been invited to manage the club because of his obvious connections? He wasn't sure. But it was a good offer anyway, so he took it. As it turned out, his connections were very useful indeed.

In December 1975 there had been rumours in the press that both Bobby Charlton and Geoff Hurst would be joining Crook on the tour. Ronnie James and Dr. Banerjee were leading the effort to secure a high profile presence on the tour and were sending off letters right, left and centre. The doctor had even managed to contact Jimmy Greaves and George Best both of whom demanded huge fees to participate. I know, I know, George Best was not in the English 1966 world cup squad but I don't believe the Indian camp would have quibbled too much about that minor point. But it was Bobby Charlton, probably England's most famous footballer, who showed most interest and appeared keenest. Perhaps it was the north-east connection but he gave every indication that he was their man.

Bobby had asked to meet representatives from the club at a Manchester hotel in November 1975. The club president, Ray Hampton, Ronnie James and Dr. Banerjee travelled to Manchester and met the great man at the Piccadilly Hotel. They lunched together before 'talking turkey', agreeing a £1000 fee and adjusting the proposed travel dates to suit the star's diary. It was a cordial, even light-hearted gathering that ended with a handshake and Bobby placing a re-assuring hand on Ronnie's shoulder:

"Don't worry. I won't let you down."

The delegation was justifiably thrilled. They had bagged one of the biggest names in world football. The journey home went that much quicker, felt that much more comfortable, could even have been described as enjoyable. When Dhiren Dey and his team received the news they were equally delighted. It was all coming together so well. But as they say in all the best westerns - it was quiet, too quiet.

As the date of the trip drew closer there were other minor details to conclude. Travelling arrangements to Heathrow airport - expenses from that point onward would be paid by the Indian hosts – overnight stays in London, new kit for the team, exchange gifts for the hosts and travel bags to present something of a professional, uniform image. A sequence of fund raising events at the club and some brass neck sponsorship appeals covered the residual costs. ATM sponsored three sets of strips with shirts specially made with a fabric designed to absorb heat and sweat and keep the players more comfortable on the park. Whether or not they were designed for temperatures over a hundred degrees is another matter. Ramar dresses supplied a kit bag for every member of the club, Rothmans supplied club pennants and a local sports shop donated a number of commemorative plaques. Arrangements were going smoothly and the crucial permission from the FA was gained after a visit by Dr. Banerjee to FA headquarters in London a month before departure. He had been received by the head man himself, Ted Croker, who passed the doctor on to a Mr. English who 'dealt with the amateurs'. An official letter was signed there and then putting the final FA seal of approval on the tour.

The team manager, Gordon Jones was faced with another task, that of finding a number of professionals to supplement the squad and add some further interest to the tour. However, the number increased as Crook regulars began to drop out of the trip, unavailable for domestic, work or other reasons. In the end nine of the Crook Town players would travel and Gordon had to find seven professionals to bring the squad up to sixteen. This was where the Jones connections worked for the club. Gordon was able to draw upon recent experience at Darlington and Middlesbrough to persuade a number of old colleagues and opponents to join the team, each for a small fee. They were, after all, professional sportsmen.

There was twenty-five year old Clive Nattress, the Darlington defender who had started his career at Blackpool and was in the middle of a seven year stint at Feethams. Then there was twenty-nine year old Scottish winger, Colin Sinclair, coming towards the end of his five year spell at Darlington after signing from Raith Rovers. Twenty four year old Eric Young, an ex-England youth international, had been a midfield apprentice at Manchester United before having spells at several clubs then finding himself at Darlington in 1974. Sedgefield born Graham Richardson was the eighteen-year old Hartlepool goalkeeper tipped for great things and twenty-nine year old Scot, George Potter was the Hartlepool full back who had arrived via, Forfar, Luton and Torquay. Gordon's ex-Middlesbrough midfield colleague and twenty one times Irish international, Eric McMordie, now at York City, also agreed to take time out and join the tour. And the final piece of the jigsaw was thirty-four year old Billy Horner, fifteen seasons a defender with Middlesbrough and Darlington and soon-to-be manager at Hartlepool. He would travel as assistant manager and player. They had many seasons of professional experience to complement the eager amateurs of Crook Town but most importantly for manager Jones, they were 'all good, honest lads who wouldn't let anyone down.' But the undoubted star attraction was England's record goal scorer and World Cup winner, Bobby Charlton.

Or so they thought. On 30th April 1976, the club received a letter from the ex-Manchester United star confirming what they had learned a couple of weeks earlier in a telephone call. Charlton had pulled out and he wanted the Crook tourists to show this letter to their Indian hosts by way of explanation and apology. Bobby had still maintained he was keen to go but had picked up an injury playing for the Irish league team, Waterford. Manager Jones was present at the home of Dr. Banerjee when the news was relayed to Dhiren Dey. The Mohun Bagan Secretary even offered £1000 for Charlton to simply turn up for the final match and wave to the crowd, but it was not going to happen. For a terrible moment, the doctor feared he may have to perform CPR down a telephone line to revive a heart attack victim in a far off continent. Shri Dey did not take the news well. Dr. Banerjee wasn't best pleased either. Other members of the organising committee were more forthright in their opinions, believing the world cup star had let them down. Yes, I think it's fair to say they were spitting stones.

This is what Bobby Charlton had to say:

April 30th/1976

Dear Sir,

       It is with much regret that due to injury I am now not able to come to Calcutta with the Crook Town F.C. I appreciate how disappointed a lot of people will be, as I am, but I still think that the remainder of the players will give the fans many enjoyable games.

       I anticipate a trip due to business, in the Far-East within the year, and I would be pleased to visit India then, and be able to see at first hand the standard of Indian Soccer which people tell me is very high.

       Dr. Brun Banerjee and all at Crook Town, have worked very hard to make this tour a great success, and being the first British side to visit India for many years, you can understand how sad I am not to be able to make the trip with them.

       Please pass on to all Indian Soccer followers - my best wishes, and when I am fit, will come to visit as soon as possible.

Yours sincerely,

Bobby Charlton.

So who were they to turn to now? They had promised their hosts an England international and World Cup star and there was precious little time to make it happen. If Gordon had been appointed for his connections, they would be tested to the limit now. As it happened, he had one trick left up his sleeve, a long standing association with Terry Paine, the ex-Southampton winger who was now playing at Hereford, bringing the curtain down on a long and distinguished career, which had included nineteen full England caps. One of those caps had come in the 2-0 victory against Mexico in the group stage of the 1966 World Cup Finals. Terry was a bone fide world cup player and member of the famous winning squad. But would he come? The answer was yes. But for how many matches would depend on Hereford's continued involvement, or otherwise, in the Welsh Cup. Nevertheless, in the worst case scenario he would be able to make it for the final game. It was a close call, but Crook had fulfilled their obligations and the tour was almost ready to roll.

The full party was:

Gordon Jones	Manager
Billy Horner	Assistant Manager
Ian Larnach	Trainer
Charlie Gott	Crook Town Centre Half and Captain
Steve Bell	Crook Town Left back
Bobby Agar	Crook Town Right Back
Charlie Morrison	Crook Town Midfield
Peter Weatherall	Crook Town Midfield
Paul Brown	Crook Town Midfield
David Pearson	Crook Town Inside Forward
Jimmy Suggett	Crook Town Winger
Terry Turnbull	Crook Town Centre Forward
Graham Richardson	Hartlepool Goalkeeper
Clive Nattress	Darlington Defender
Colin Sinclair	Darlington Inside Forward
Eric Young	Darlington Midfield
Eric McMordie	York City Midfield
George Potter	Hartlepool Full Back

Accompanying the players would be Dr. Banerjee , his wife, two boys and secretary Freda, club chairman Wilf Collingwood and wife Elsie, tour secretary Ronnie James and wife Jenny, treasurer Herbert Hutchinson and his wife and kit man Jimmy Gibson. To complete the party, Pat and Margaret Partridge would join the team at Heathrow and Terry Paine would join them in India when his Hereford commitments were completed. Finally, and you've got to admire their dedication, there was a small number of supporters so excited at the prospect of seeing their team in such an exotic setting, they paid their own way to India to witness the tour.

All done. Dr. Banerjee had even personally overseen the necessary jabs prior to travelling to the Indian sub-continent – it's handy having a doctor on the committee. Poor old Terry Turnbull was convinced he actually had full blown malaria after the jabs. The rest of the team said nothing to disabuse him of the notion, of course. They were ready to travel and ready for action. The tour that grew from a chance comment over a pint of ale was almost under way. All they had to do was get to Heathrow airport on Saturday 1st May.

Garlands and Greetings

Not since 1727 had Britain seen a year like it. The summer of 1976 was hot. Oh, it was hot. And it was dry. I mean rock hard, shrivelled and crunchy. The Thames crisped up at its source in Gloucestershire and in London was at its lowest level in living memory. Reservoirs became cracked, arid plains and hosepipe bans and water rationing were introduced. The front lawn was wispy brown stubble and sunburn was the fashion of the day. Everywhere you looked, big red faces stared back at you with hideously peeling noses and sun-bleached hair. Roads were littered with hissing and steaming cars, radiators over-heating and grinding to a nineteen seventies halt. Students spent the early summer revising and preparing for exams by playing tennis and watching the cricket while normal people worked with sweat stained shirts and loosened kipper ties. Clowns like me went walking and camping in the Lake District with friends and spent two weeks drinking fresh, unpasteurised milk, cool, eye-closingly refreshing dry cider and the last, apologetic trickles of what used to be mountain streams. People were dying out there in our long, hot summer while we were getting high on Cavray's pork sausages and Strongbow.

Perhaps Harold Wilson had seen it all coming. He stunned the political world by resigning as prime minister on March 16th. It was a mystery to everyone except Harold. He reckons he had agreed with Mary that when he reached sixty he'd quit. Well, he did and James Callaghan became the British Premier on 5th April. Wilson was obviously a keen amateur weather forecaster who had foreseen a cracking summer and decided it was too good to miss. Bird watching in the Scilly Isles would be a tad more enjoyable than appointing ministers for drought and trying to stay cool in cabinet.

This was also the year that Manchester United made a comeback to the big time by reaching the FA Cup Final for the first time in thirteen years. It was their first chance of a major honour since the European Cup triumph in 1968. They were up against Southampton, a small time second division outfit pulled together by a big time Geordie, ex-guardsman who had managed Bishop Auckland. Lawrie McMenamy had contrived to raise mediocre players above their own expectations and revive one or two flagging careers by giving them fresh belief. The mix was potent and the result was a 'predictable shock'. Southampton acquired their one and only major trophy and 'Big Lawrie' was a hero.

Watching the game at Wembley that day, Saturday May 1st, were Bobby Charlton and Pat Partridge. Bobby, recently resigned from his post as manager at Preston North End, was hired for TV to give expert summary and analysis while Pat, England's top official, was a guest of the FA as the previous year's final referee. Both men had been approached by Crook Town to travel with them on their Indian adventure but only one would join the team at Heathrow airport the following day. Pat was accompanied by his wife Margaret who also had a return ticket to Calcutta in her purse.

Back in the north-east, sixteen players and assorted officials and management staff were neatly folding their underpants and having a final hair cut before setting off on their journey down the A1 to London. They would spend Saturday night at a Heathrow hotel and have a 'good night on the pop' ahead of the marathon flight to Calcutta. Listening to Radio One whilst ironing their socks, the expectant travellers were treated to The Brotherhood of Man chirruping the current number one hit record, 'Save All Your Kisses For Me'. This was followed by Fernando, the latest release from Abba, which would knock them off the top spot a week from now. Yes, the same Abba who shamelessly aped the career of the legendary B.O.M by lining up with two birds and two blokes and utilising Latino Christian names for song titles. Who could forget the jaw-dropping Angelo and the ground-breaking Figaro by 'The Brotherhoods'. Abba then had the gall to attempt to distinguish themselves from the original article by making their birds good looking and their blokes talented. Typical Swedes.

So it was that at ten o'clock on morning of the 1st May 1976, an excited and expectant coach pulled away from Crook market place with the first contingent of the touring party onboard. The Crook based members of the party were joined by those from south Durham at Stockton and the final pick up was at Scotch Corner, the very symbol of the Great North Road. A building, a location, a name that evokes the very spirit of being 'on the road'. Each stop and pick up was greeted by huge cheers from those already onboard. There was singing, the obligatory card games and a tingle of anticipation. But the anticipation was of a good time, a special and unusual tour. No-one on the bus really believed that what they were about to embark upon was anything more than a slightly better version of the usual post-season break. Some of the Crook team had not even travelled, unable or unwilling to take two weeks away from work. What actually lay ahead was beyond anything they could have imagined.

The only members of the touring party not on the coach that morning were

Pat and Margaret Partridge who had stayed over night in London ahead of the historic May Day Cup Final and of course, the star turn, Terry Paine. After the final whistle, Bobby Charlton had given his headphones back to the BBC and was headed off to allow an injured knee to recuperate instead of jetting off to Calcutta to expose his head to the searing heat of the Indian sun. As for Pat and Margaret, well they were seasoned travellers because of Pat's overseas refereeing assignments. Fully aware of the possibilities of Delhi belly and other intestinal nasties that a change of water can induce, Margaret had packed a healthy stock of her cure-all, or should I say, prevent-all, digestive biscuits. Get something dry and bland on your stomach and you'll be all right.

The bus party and the Partridge family finally came together on Sunday afternoon at Heathrow Airport. Bored but excited, they kicked their heels in the normal airport way as they awaited the departure of their Air India flight bound for Calcutta via the East Indian capital of Maharashtra, Bombay, or as it is known today, Mumbai. Most of the professionals were used to foreign excursions but many of the tourists were new to the travel game. Some were apprehensive about the flight. Others were frankly, bricking it. Worst of all was big centre forward, Terry Turnbull, a man about to leave the ground for the first time in his life. All shoulders, beard and lots of black hair, this was a man who looked like he would spit in the eye of the devil and tell him that tridents are for poofs. However, the thought of heading skywards and looking down at the world from twenty-five thousand feet had him quivering like Pavarotti's belly after a good slap. Sucking a barley sugar certainly wasn't going to help.

Luggage checked in and passports at the ready, the gang left the terminal building to cross the tarmac towards their transport for the day, one of those new-fangled Jumbo Jets, the Boeing 747. In one final gesture before rising from British turf, they all lined up for a tour photograph in front of the giant craft. Sponsored kit bags to the fore, the party assembled for the lens with a fantastic assortment of wing collars, mutton-chop side burns, flared trousers and facial hair from the 'Age of Aquarius'. It's tempting to say it wasn't a pretty sight but we all looked like that in 1976.

Once aboard it was 'chocks away' and prepare for take-off. The India trip had begun in earnest. The giant air plane lumbered down the runway and slowly, almost miraculously to the layman's eye, clawed its way skyward before levelling off high above the weather and extinguishing the seat belt signs. Amidst the excitement and anticipation, Terry Turnbull ('Big T' to his mates), a major bag of nerves, was taken under the worldly wing of Pat and Margaret Partridge. They sat next to him, one either side, trying to imbue some confidence, even holding his hands for comfort and solidarity. But try as they might, big Terry was a basket case.

"Oh, God. This is bloody awful."

"Just relax Terry. Loosen your tie… Go on, that's right. Undo your shoelaces. It's fine. It's perfectly safe. Unfasten your safety belt….come on now…slowly does it."

"No, no. It's a safety belt. It's meant to be fastened."

"You can release it now. It's fine. Come on. Stand up. Have a walk around. I'll come with you."

The tour party leaving Heathrow on 2nd May 1976. Dr. Banerjee has clearly been watching Dallas on TV.

"This is not natural. It's just not natural."

"Come on. Look out of the window....You can manage it."

"Oh, bloody hell....hold on....hold on."

While Terry fought back the fear of falling from the sky and Pat and Margaret played Good Samaritan, the drinks trolley was doing brisk business. Most of the players were keen to have a relaxing drink. One or two saw greater possibilities. Gordon Jones, the tour manager, was sitting next to old friend and team mate, Eric McMordie. Eric had first been introduced to English football as one of two Belfast boys on trial at Manchester United. Famously, they were so shy and homesick that they were back on the ferry home after one day. The other boy was George Best. Perhaps not surprisingly, Eric liked a drink. So it did come as something of a shock that as Gordon ordered a half of beer from the trolley his old friend settled for a half of orange cordial. What the manager didn't realise was that Eric had stashed a bottle of gin in his kit bag. When the trolley dolly had moved to a safe distance down the isle, Eric reached up to the luggage compartment, brought down the bag and proceeded to zip and unzip it at regular intervals, smuggling out the gin to top up the orange. It was a gradual process but it's fair to say that he got pissed.

The Jumbo couldn't make it to Bombay in one hop so it had to have a pit stop in Dubai for re-fuelling. The passengers were allowed to disembark in order to stretch legs and get a change of scenery. However, one of their number stayed onboard. Conscious of the fact that Dubai was a dry state, Eric had a sudden attack of the panics and figured he'd be in big trouble if officials spotted that he'd been at the bottle. Fearing imminent arrest and possible incarceration in a cockroach infested prison, he would surely end his days eating stale bread and gruel, scratching the names of close family members onto hot, stained cell walls and catching glimpses of the desert sky through a tiny, barred window high above his head. He'd never see a gin and orange again. To make dam sure this didn't happen he stuck to his seat and enjoyed a liquid fuelled, solitary reverie while the others tried to find something remotely interesting in a Dubai airport shop. In these two tasks, Eric was by some distance, the more successful.

After ten hours on the wing, the flight landed at Bombay where there was a transfer onto an internal Indian flight to Calcutta. 'Big T' had just about conquered his nerves on the Jumbo Jet, a craft that cuts a swathe through the air and takes no shit from turbulence. However, the twin-prop, wing-flapper that took them on their onward journey brought back the demons and the big centre forward was once again left gripping his seat and saying his prayers. The final leg of the journey took the total travel time to sixteen hours. The travellers were tired and weary and anxious to get to the hotel as soon as possible. But, disembarking at Calcutta airport on Monday morning was not quite what they had expected. On descending the air plane steps, it became clear that there were large numbers of people waiting in anticipation of an arrival. Someone famous perhaps? Someone important perhaps? Well, who's to say who is important and who is not? On this occasion they were the VIPs. They were whisked past customs, somewhat dazed by the attention, and into the eager clutches of a massive, cheering, spellbound crowd who were there to greet and welcome the famous Crook Town..... and the legendary Bobby Charlton. The shock of the welcome was like a jug of cold water thrown at their sleepy faces. They were bestowed with a sudden and unexpected vitality as banners and flags were waved, cameras flashed, shirt sleeves were touched, hands were eagerly grasped and shaken, backs were slapped and the crowd throbbed as, what can only be described as 'Crook mania' gripped the people. And, of course, the media were to the fore. The media? Why on earth were press, television and radio there to greet a post season tour of a Northern League team?

"Which one is Bobby Charlton?"

"Who is the manager?"

"How do you like India?"

"Can we have an interview?"

The questions rang out from all quarters.

"Wait, wait. You must all come through me." An Irish accent could be heard above the chaos. *"I'm Mr. Jones' personal assistant. All requests must come through me."*

Eric McMordie may have been drunk but he was smiling and he was loving it.

Further honour was to bestowed on the visitors when out of the frenzied welcome party leapt a posse of garland wielding locals who proceeded to adorn each of the bewildered guests of the country. For that is exactly how this tour was being perceived in Calcutta. These people were guests of the whole country. Players who were used to trotting out before a hundred people at Tow Law and having their results recorded in the local press beside the darts and dominoes league were now being paraded before the media of the worlds largest democracy. Chief amongst the welcome party was Dhiren Dey, the Secretary of the Mohun Bagan Athletic Club and a celebrated all-rounder for the club's cricket team in the 1930s and 40s. It took about two minutes to realise that this was bigger than anything they had ever imagined. A brief session of interviews in the VIP lounge was handled, in the main, by the proud and particular Dr. Banerjee. Thrust into the spotlight and fluent in Hindi, he was able and more than willing, to respond to the greetings.

Dhiren Dey presents Jimmy Suggett with his garland on arrival at Calcutta Airport.

With the cheers of welcome still ringing in their ears, the party was swept along to a waiting convoy of taxis ready to transport them to their accommodation. It was during this happy, flurry of activity that the best of human behaviour was juxtaposed to the worst. Chairman, Wilf Collingwood and wife, Elsie were inexplicably and disastrously separated from the rest of the party and man-handled by the only two people in Calcutta airport who didn't seem to be wearing a smile and bearing a garland. They were expertly relieved of anything of any potential value and left stranded, bemused, frightened, shaken and confused as the wonderful welcome turned horribly sour. The old couple was re-united with the rest of the party, police were informed and they were helped into one of the taxis, which would take them to the safety and comfort of their hotel. The very lowest moment of the tour came right at the beginning. Wilf and Elsie would take some time to recover their composure but the whole party and the hosts rallied round to ensure the rest of their visit would be characterised by kindness and generosity.

Home for the duration of their stay in Calcutta would be the Oberoi Grand, a model of Victorian splendour and opulence. The Indian hosts had pulled out all the stops. This was hospitality of the highest order. Dr. Banerjee was well aware of the significance.

> *"This is the biggest and finest hotel in the whole of Calcutta. Five stars. It is the most aristocratic by far."*

Situated on Chowringhee Road on the eastern edge of The Maidan, the vast green wedge known as the 'lungs' of Calcutta, Oberoi is a place to be pampered. Tasteful and immaculate, it was the sort of jaw-dropping accommodation that most of the Crooksters would only have experienced watching films about rich people going to stay in India – if such a film exists. Three restaurants, an outdoor pool, palm tree courtyard, rooms of sheer, unrelenting luxury – most impressively for the lads – each with its own bar and of course the obligatory Indian servants. In addition, the host club, Mohun Bagan had arranged for the players to receive, what can only be described as pocket money, which they were asked to use rather than changing sterling. Why? Who knows. But there you are, no-one was arguing. If Ronnie, Gordon, Terry, Eric, Charlie and co. had not realised from the reception at the airport that this was a tour out of the ordinary, then they did now.

After being paired off by the manager in true 'rooming' fashion, the players and accompanying guests enjoyed a brief respite to settle into their accomodation. After bouncing on the beds, marvelling at the bar, running around the bathroom, feeling the pile on the carpets and exclaiming, "have you seen this view?" it was time for a pre-dinner press conference. A bloody press conference! OK, so the newspapers had heard about the visit and wanted a few quotes from the tourists. Manager, Gordon Jones, organised and meticulous, was asked to front the conference with (more or less) sober, senior professional and Northern Irish international Eric McMordie, captain Charlie Gott and de-facto assistant manager, Billy Elliot. As they entered the sparkling ballroom to face the press a small army of media types greeted them with a volley of flashing bulbs and a demanding row of microphones lined up on the top table. When their eyes began to see what they were looking at, around three hundred faces were staring back. Each attached to a journalist with a camera, a note pad or a microphone. Gordon Jones was stunned.

"I feel like bloody Matt Busby, Eric."

"Don't get carried away."

The gentle interrogation lasted about an hour. Thankfully, in a room cooled by large, sweeping fans.

"So what do you think of India, Mr. Jones?" – (Don't know, only been here five minutes)

"What do you know of football in our country?" – (Bugger all)

"We are disappointed that Bobby Charlton cannot be with us. However, we are looking forward to welcoming world cup star, Terry Paine. What can you tell the people of Calcutta about Mr. Paine?" – (He's not bald – ah, so you all know Bobby's not coming)

The four exhausted and shell-shocked celebrities retired to their rooms, exiting the press conference through an admiring throng. All they wanted now was a quiet drink and the chance to sit down and make some sense of a headful of words and pictures that had gathered throughout this astonishing day. Billy and Charlie, rooming together headed off for some peace and quiet but were interrupted by a voice calling across the hotel foyer.

"Charlie? Charlie Gott? Is that you?"

"Brian? What the hell are you doing here? I didn't come all the way to Calcutta to meet my next door neightbour!"

Brian Peacock, Charlie's old neighbour from his early days in Thornley, Co. Durham was working in Calcutta and staying in the Oberoi Grand. Cue much hand shaking and incredulous comments and talk of a small world.

However, Eric and Gordon received a surprise of their own when they reached their room and found an Indian boy of about nineteen seated quietly outside their door. They looked at one another, thought little more of it and went inside to crack a drink. After a short while, curiosity overtook the pair and they decided to take a peak outside the door. He was still there. As they stepped into the corridor, the boy stood respectfully and looked at them both as if awaiting instruction.

"Hello, son. Can we help you?"

No response.

"Is there something wrong?"

"No sahib. I am for you."

Gordon and Eric faced each other with a mixture of shock and mild amusement then shifted uneasily.

"Aye, aye...what's all this? I think you've got the wrong room son."

"No sahib. I am for you. I am here to help you. If you need anything I will take care that you are served."

"Oh,...right...oh, well that's alright then. Excellent....Good lad."

"I am here to help."

Two footballers, one servant, one mini-bar. Well, if they'd been in Crook they would have offered him a drink. They weren't used to this servant thing. Eric stepped in.

"I'll tell y' what. Come in and have a drink. C'mon. What's you're name? I'm Eric, this is Gordon."

"I'm Kamal, sahib. But I cannot take a drink with you. I am here to serve."

"Get away lad. You're here to do as we say, right?"

"That is right."

"Okay. We want you to come in for a drink. We'd be offended if you refused."

And so it was that Kamal was introduced to the mini-bar that his status in life would have never allowed. He would travel everywhere with the party, fetch drinks, order taxis and generally do the bidding of his temporary masters. For his troubles, Eric and Gordon smuggled him into their room to sleep on the floor instead of a chair outside the door. Kamal was having a whale of a time. And why not?

It's not cricket - but still they came

In 1756, the activities of the British traders became too much for the local Indian ruler, Siraj-ud-duala, the Nawab of Murshidabad, who had watched with apprehension as the British factories took on an increasingly permanent and fortified appearance. Their influence was growing too fast and spreading too far. A largely muslim army, under his leadership, attacked the town, driving out most of the British. Those that remained were captured and packed into an underground cellar where, during the night, most of them suffocated and died in what became known as 'the black hole of Calcutta'. Six months later, a relief mission under the leadership of Robert Clive (Of India) recaptured control of the town by using a renegade Indian general who turned against the Nawab. Calcutta was under British control again and they were not about to let it slip from their grasp this time.

They set about a massive jungle clearance after re-locating the inhabitants of the village of Govindpur and laid the foundations for a new fort to replace the original Fort William on a key strategic site next to a bend on the Hooghly river. Work began in 1758 and was not complete until 1781. It was a massive project giving the fort a huge expanse of open space around it in order that cannons would have a clear line of fire to defend the town. The fort has never fired a single shot in anger since its completion. The vast area cleared around the fort, three kilometres by one, became known as The Maidan. To the south of The Maidan are the racecourse, polo ground and Victoria Memorial. To the north-west corner is Eden Gardens.

Named after the sister of the former governor general, Lord Auckland, Eden Gardens are small but beautiful. Adorned with a Burmese pagoda set in an elegantly picturesque lake and a short stroll from the banks of the lumbering Hooghly, the gardens are also home to the Ranji Stadium or Calcutta Cricket Ground. However, it is better known to the sporting world simply as Eden Gardens, one of the biggest and most historic test cricket venues in the world. At 4.00pm on May 4th 1976, Crook Town was scheduled to play the first game of their post-season tour against the host Mohun Bagan Club at Eden Gardens. They were expecting a decent crowd. After all, this was the first ever football game at the famous cricket stadium and there had been a deluge of media attention.

The team had been allocated a training time of 2.00pm on Monday 3rd May at the stadium itself. A good opportunity to get acclimatised to the ground and the heat. The problem was that at over 110 degrees the word hot didn't quite do justice to the overbearing, suffocating temperature. Fearing that training in such conditions may do more harm than good, particularly with a certain amount of jet lag hanging over the team, manager Jones decided that a light session followed by a more relaxed approach was appropriate. So it was that the boys spent the afternoon by the pool, taking the occasional dip, reading the odd book and telling the odd joke. But there was strictly no alcohol. In fact, they were very well behaved. Preparation for the first game was being taken seriously. There was a degree of excitement and expectation building in the camp. In Calcutta itself, unknown to the team, the clamour for tickets was extraordinary. It seemed that the whole city wanted one. The anticipation of this historic game was at fever pitch. But as they sipped and snoozed in the Oberoi Grand, the players were blissfully unaware that Crook versus Mohun Bagan was the only show in town.

An early night (preceded by a night cap for some) was followed by breakfast in one of the three sumptuous restaurants and a morning spent relaxing in and around the hotel. However, one or two of the more inquisitive members of the party ventured out for a stroll to capture some of the atmosphere of the streets. The centre of the city was neat, tidy and dominated by the characteristic white buildings and general hubbub but there was an unexpected buzz. It soon became apparent that the Crook players were the cause of that buzz. Once recognised, they were hounded – respectfully of course - for tickets and offered all kinds of 'remuneration' for them. They had been burdened with instant celebrity and a level of respect they were unlikely to receive from the Millfield Ground faithful on a wet and windy Saturday afternoon in February after a 0-0 draw with Horden Colliery. With the growing realisation of what this tour meant to the people of Calcutta the light lunch was liberally sprinkled with an exotic spice known as trepidation. The amateur members of the squad and the organising committee in particular were just anxious not to disappoint – or worse.

On the short taxi journey to Eden Gardens the entourage picked its way through the usual melee of old fumey cars, rickshaws and oxen. Horns sounded, brakes screeched, voices shouted out and the cattle pulling carts loaded with sacks and cartons and boxes, shat on the street. Beggars begged, markets traded and vivid colours splashed across the city in a defiant celebration of life. This was Calcutta in all its exhilarating, bewildering normality. But there was clearly something extra in the air. They arrived at the ground one hour before kick-off and Eden Gardens was already completely full with thousands unable to get into the ground. And when Eden Gardens is full that means one hundred thousand people.

The squad was led to the famous pavilion changing rooms with huge fans beating the air above their heads like giant birds of prey. The rooms tingled with the spirit of the great cricketers, past and present, who had slipped into their whites, padded up, adjusted a box or sat slumped in dejection after an early dismissal. The great centurions of Eden Gardens, West Indies' Kanhai in 1958, England's Cowdrey in 1963, New Zealand's Sutcliffe in 1964 had all returned to those changing rooms with bats raised in acknowledgement of an appreciative crowd. Yet here they were, nine northern league amateurs from Crook and six guest professionals about to walk out into that same arena. The arena that usually echoed to the sound of a cover drive flashing from a wooden blade to the boundary rope. Or a skid and a thud as a strike bowler launches a quickie that fizzes past the bat and into the outstretched, gloved hands of the wicket keeper. Or the pitter patter of polite applause as an average innings comes to an uneventful end.

Referee, Pat Partridge was ushered into a separate area sectioned off by screens with a number of hand-picked Indian officials from whom he could choose his linesmen for the game. To say they were in awe of him was like saying Marilyn Monroe was a tidy bird who acted in a couple of feature films. Officiating standards were not high in Indian football and the man in their midst was one of the world's best. They treated him like a god and Pat treated them and the game with every respect. He regarded himself as a representative of the FA and was determined that the Indian public would see a top class refereeing performance as well as a good game of football. As Pat and the players undertook their pre-match preparations, a band of Indian musicians in dhotis serenaded them with shehnai, mridangan and sitar. The hosts had made every effort to create an atmosphere that represented their culture.

"These musicians were sitting cross legged in white robes playing weird snake charmer music while we got changed." Clearly the influence of Asian music had not permeated the record collections of Crook.

In time honoured fashion, the players were invited onto the pitch well before kick-off to inspect the playing surface and sample the atmosphere. This is the part where cup final teams wander aimlessly around the pitch with their hands in the pockets of specially tailored suits surveying the crowd and waving to points on the terraces approximating to where their families are seated. This was when the first wave of disbelief hit them. After all, these people had come to see Crook Town. This crowd was as big as an English Cup Final, as big as the biggest Indian test match, as big as the World Cup Final ten years earlier. It was quite literally, unbelievable. At least this baptism meant that the shock wouldn't be quite so acute when they walked onto the field to start the game.

The other members of the touring party were led to the Eden Gardens equivalent of the Directors' Box to watch the game with the other invited dignitaries. And it is a fact that India does 'dignitaries' even better than the English. "Don't stand on ceremony" is not a saying in India. Acting Secretary, Ronnie James was also invited by the Indian club officials to inspect the field before the match. They were proud of the surface they had produced and were anxious for members of the organising committee to see it at first hand. The pitch was marked out in the centre of the huge green expanse and did not respect the boundaries of the test wicket. Today it was a football pitch and cricket was a distant memory. If they roughed up the bowlers' end a bit, it was tough. As Ronnie, shirt sleeved but smart as a carrot, strolled out to the middle with his hosts, an excitement rose from within the huge crowd. A flurry of applause and appreciation rippled around the stadium at the site of Ronnie James – from behind. He turned, slightly bemused and gave a faintly embarrassed wave. It was indeed Ronnie who had caused the flap. He inspected the field, which was like a bowling green and walked slowly back to take his seat accompanied by yet more applause. The others couldn't contain their laughter as he slipped back into his place.

"What was all that about?…What's up?….What's going on?"

"They think you're Bobby Charlton."

"What do you mean, Bobby Charlton. I look nowt like him. Any way, he's not here."

"You do from here….with that head. Word mustn't have got round everyone yet."

The Crook team seem to be encountering great difficulty in lining up before the game against Mohun Bagan. They are, from left to right, Eric Young, Charlie Gott, Clive Nattress, Graham Richardson, Bobby Agar, Paul Brown (1/2 head), Colin Sinclair (too far back), Terry Turnbull, George Potter. Front: Steve Bell, Jimmy Suggett, Charlie Morrison, Eric McMordie (with mascot Anindo Banerjee), Billy Horner, Peter Weatherell

Back in the dressing room the team took their final orders from Manager Jones and Billy Horner. They had already struck an agreement with Mohun Bagan that because of the intense heat they could use as many substitutes as necessary. It was even agreed that players could return to the pitch after being replaced. They were instructed to play a holding game and attempt to score on the break. It was important to conserve energy as the opposition would be far more used to the conditions than Crook.

The two teams lined up side by side before the grand entrance. The tourists were in their usual amber shirts and black shorts with the hosts in their famous maroon and racing green vertical halves. The club had chosen the colours of the Durham Light Infantry who were influential in their formation in 1889. Much nervous shuffling and deep breathing was in evidence as the teams waited to be introduced by the public address system before beginning the short walk into the blinding sunlight and searing mid-afternoon heat. Captain, Charlie Gott would have the additional stress of conducting the introductions to the dignitaries so, being less familiar with the faces of the guest professionals, decided to put names to faces by memorising their position in the line up. Walking onto the pitch it was like opening the oven door to check your Yorkshire puddings. Only this time, the blast was accompanied by a huge, deafening cheer from the expectant crowd. It's a certainty that nobody's Yorkshires have ever had such a reception. The players walked slowly towards the position designated for the official line up. Their eyes scanned the massive arena, heaving with joyous Indians packed into the stands. Lumps came to throats and lips were licked dry as nerves kicked in and the enormity of the occasion dawned. Where the seating areas were not so high, tree tops around the outside of the perimeter of the stadium could be seen filled with eager and adventurous locals clinging to the branches in order to catch a glimpse of the visiting heroes. The second wave of disbelief crashed onto the Crook shoreline. At this stage even the hoary old pros were seized by the magnitude of the moment. Most of them had never encountered a crowd like this in a combined eighty years in the professional game.

The invited guests and dignitaries, including President of the National Congress, Mr. Dev Kanta Barua, Chief Minister for sport, Mr. Siddharta Sankar Ray and Advocate General and President of the IFA, Mr. Gauri Nath Mitra were presented to the players, Dr. Banerjee and Ronnie James. Young Anindo Banerjee, team mascot and son of the doctor was also on hand for the team photograph and the coin toss. Once again, it was a 'camera fest' for the press. Unfortunately for Charlie, the players had swapped positions for the line up. His grand memory plan was scuppered. He found himself staring at faces whose names he simply couldn't recall. He had to think fast.

> *"This is Bobby Agar, David Pearson... er, Mr. Michael Mouse. Charlie Morrison, Steve Bell... er, Mr. Donald Duck..."*

The rest of the line up had to exercise maximum personal restraint to prevent themselves from cracking up.

The crowning glory of the opening ceremony came when the teams, armed with specially prepared bouquets, were asked to disperse to all corners of the stadium to throw the flowers to the crowd. The fans went wild. Clearly bouquets are popular in Calcutta. As the Amrita Bazar Patrika newspaper put it the following day:

> **'There was no dearth of arrangements that usually lend colour to the inauguration of such sports events with international flavour.'**

Indeed, the 'Patrika' as I shall refer to it, lent its own shades of colour to the rest of the tour with an idiosyncratic style of prose and artistic turn of phrase that revived memories of another age.

Pat Partridge called the two captains to the middle to spin the coin and exchange club emblems. Captain, Charlie Gott stepped up for Crook and Prasanta Mitra for Mohun Bagan. Then, after the pitch was cleared of the VIPs, the whistle sounded and Mohun Bagan began the first game of the tour to the backdrop of another huge roar from the crowd. The first ever football match in the Eden Gardens' Ranji stadium was played out between the following two teams:

Crook Town AFC: 4-4-2

G. Richardson;

C. Nattress   C. Gott   G. Potter   S. Bell;

P. Brown   E. Young   E. McMordie   C. Morrison;

C. Sinclair   T. Turnbull

Substitute appearances: Horner, Weatherall, Suggett and Agar

Mohun Bagan: 4-2-4

Prasanta Mitra

Dilip Sarkar   Subrata Bhattacharjee   P. Chowdhury   Dilip Palit

Samaresh Chowdhury   Rasun Banerjee

Ulaganathan   Akbar   Habib   Subhas Bhowmick

The Mohun team was of a standard roughly equivalent to today's Nationwide Conference. So with a Northern League team supplemented by a sprinkling of experienced league professionals, the teams were very evenly matched. The pace was predictably slow and Crook pursued their game plan to contain the opposition and hit them on the break.

> *'In such conditions, it was quite obvious that the English team could not bring those qualities and circumspection that were expected of them, to the game.'*   **The 'Patrika'**

Mohun were playing some neat and tidy stuff. Lovely football in fact. And though they were diminutive there was no doubting they were 'hard little buggers'. They also had a philosophy that football should be played on the floor and proceeded to knock it around with consummate ease. However, they rarely threatened Graham Richardson in the Crook goal.

> '...but his manners suggested that he was a high class custodian.'
> **The 'Patrika'**

The experienced 'stopper-backs', Nattress and Potter marshalled the defence and captain Gott had a brilliant game as they continued to cut out any danger and either feed the midfield or attempt the long ball up to big centre forward, Terry Turnbull. This tactic puzzled the Indian hosts and the intrigued crowd who had never seen anything quite like it. Mohun Bagan had lined up 4-2-4 but were playing in the old 2-3-5 formation favoured in pre-historic England and still coached by one teacher in one outpost of County Durham until the early seventies – personal experience can testify to that fact. Today we might call their approach naïve. But I won't because that would be a tired old cliché. However, their system did lack a certain maturity, shall we say. Nevertheless, they were entertaining and skilful but lacked a killer instinct in front of goal because of,

> 'The almost traditional infirmities of the players ....'
> **The 'Patrika' – again.**

The game continued at a relatively leisurely pace but it was competitive and challenges were by no means half-hearted. Charlie Morrison had tested the resolve of the Indians when he hit their sweeper, Bhattacharjee, early in the game with a crunching tackle. He also discovered they had learned some English when the defender responded with, "You bastard." However, on occasions it had the air of an exhibition match but would snap into life with a lunge forward, a flying tackle or a piece of individual skill. Crook raised the temperature by taking the lead through Colin Sinclair six minutes after the break when the Darlington forward pounced upon a poor clearance and capitalised on hesitant goalkeeping to slot the ball into an empty net.

> 'Crook Town scored their goal mainly due to some unpardonable lapses on the part of the Mohun Bagan defenders.'
>
> **The 'Patrika'**

The equaliser came with only thirteen minutes remaining after Mohun had wasted several good chances and the Crook players began to sag in the heat. Habib latched on to a Dilip Sarkar lob and found himself within a 'measurable distance from goal' from where he beat Richardson with a low, left-footer into the corner. Habib, one of Indian football's true stars, would play against Crook on four occasions during the tour and earn the admiration of his opponents for his strength, skill and flair. There's no doubt he could have 'cut the mustard' in England. Both goals were greeted with equal enthusiasm by a sporting and even handed crowd. However, the biggest cheers of the afternoon were reserved for Charlie 'Tosser' Morrison. Now you can speculate, if you must, on how Charlie came about that nickname. The truth is, he had one hell of a throw on him. A throw in from 'Tosser' (you see, he 'tossed' the ball a long way) was equivalent to a corner or free kick and the football mad crowd had never before seen such a spectacle. He became an instant folk hero and every throw was greeted like a cup final winner in the last minute of injury time. Just the sight of Charlie wiping his hands whilst bending down to pick up the ball was enough to send the spectators into raptures. Local newspapers were so taken by the 'Tosser phenomenon' that he was the subject of numerous cartoons. Eden Gardens had seen many a ball tossed in from the boundary, but never one as big as this.

Manager Jones used four substitutes one of whom, Billy Horner, came on early in the game for the unfortunate Paul Brown. The Crook midfielder collapsed with dehydration soon after the start. He was fine after drinking a barrel of water and being administered to by Dr. Banerjee but it soon became obvious that playing a full ninety minutes outfield was not recommended. In fact, an agreement was immediately reached that future games would only be eighty minutes duration and manager Jones would utilise a full squad rotation policy. Poor old Pat Partridge had no such luxury though. Such was his god-like status amongst the Indian officials, no-one had the confidence to step into his shoes and give him a break. When he finally blew for the end of the game, a good rest well earned, the two teams shook hands to the rhythm of a thunderous ovation from the Eden Gardens crowd. Amid the mutual congratulations and shirt swapping, it was big Terry Turnbull who bagged the prized Habib number nine shirt that frankly, looks as if it could have been purchased from the junior bargain rack at the local sports warehouse. But in this case, something very good came in a little bundle. The game had been an overwhelming success and Ronnie James' fears of under performance, even humiliation, were swept aside. Crook had performed admirably and one hundred thousand people left a famous old cricket stadium having witnessed Indian sporting history – and the biggest tosser in town.

The dressing room was a good place to be. The players were understandably high on the experience and proud to have been part of the occasion. They had performed well and been greeted like superstars. The Mohun Bagan dressing room was equally elated and for similar reasons. However, they were puzzled by the English tactics and were keen to learn why Crook had used the long ball, which was so unfamiliar to them. It was left to manager Jones to explain to them that December in Britain didn't produce conditions quite like May in India. Mohun Bagan was not used to playing on mud. Nor were they used to the English boots, which attracted a lot of interest and some offers of purchase following the final whistle.

The team returned to the hotel, shattered and pleased with their efforts but now that the people had seen them play their status had risen even further. Fans and snappers followed them everywhere. Autographs, photographs and requests for tickets for future matches were routine. But once back at the Oberoi Grand it was a night for a drink. Tomorrow was a rest day. However, there was one further duty for the manager and the young goalkeeper Graham Richardson. They were invited to a local radio station to be interviewed. Gordon because he had become the spokesman for the group and Graham because he was an English under 19 international and at eighteen years old, the baby of the party. Only Anindo Banerjee was younger but then again, he was the mascot. There were the predictable questions about how the game went and how much the tourists were enjoying India and the odd probing enquiry about the future of the Indian game.

"So, Mr. Jones. How do you think our football in India could be improved?

"Get some floodlights."

"I don't understand. Can you explain?"

"You need to play in the evening. It's too hot out here. You can only play in the evening if you have lights."

"Ah, very good Mr. Jones. Very good."

It wasn't meant to be a joke but it would be around fifteen years before someone twigged that lights would indeed be a good idea.

Most of the squad made good use of the hotel bar facilities that evening. It was not a time to celebrate but it was certainly a time to relax. However, the management of the Oberoi Grand was not in quite the same munificent mood as the host club and tour organisers had been. In short, they insisted that everyone must pay for their drinks. After all, the visitors had been given spending money – sorry – out of pocket expenses for the trip. But manager Jones was not too happy about this.

"We've just played in a stadium packed with a hundred thousand spectators who all paid for tickets. Somebody's making something out of this, so I think that a few free drinks wouldn't be out of order. Pay for nowt. You sign for the drinks lads. We'll settle up later."

Sixteen thirsty footballers with a free drinks tab. May 4th just got even better.

Things to do in Calcutta when you're NOT playing football

After the monumental high of the first tour match the players were encouraged to relax on the rest day before the next fixture on the 6th May. It was a chance to get out and see something of the host city or simply enjoy an easy day around the pool. Spirits were high after the unforgettable experiences of the previous day. Of the squad, only Bobby Agar and Steve Bell were feeling particularly home sick and ready for a more familiar weather forecast. But it didn't stop them joining the rest of the players lying out on the pool surround, each with a little drinks table replete with an automatic flag which, at the touch of a button, would rise up its own mini flag pole. As the flag rose, one of a row of waiting servants would rush to attendance.

"My round chaps," would be the cry from the table. "Twenty four rum and cokes."

It's amazing how generous a person becomes when there is a free bar. It's equally amazing how competitive a person can become after taking advantage of said bar. Swimming competitions were the order of the day. Racing lengths for a small wager was an interesting diversion. In this particular activity it was not one of the players who excelled but Dr. Banerjee. He took on all-comers and skinned them.

"He was like a bloody slick shark. He skimmed across the water."

What the players hadn't realised was that the doctor had been a swimming champion as a student and had retained a good deal of this prowess into this, his forty-third year.

But non-football time was not just eaten up by holiday activity. Such was the impact of the visit, they weren't released from official duties that included hospital visits to bring smiles to the faces of sick children. Now this is the sort of image you might normally associate with Princess Diana, the People's Princess. Or even Roger Moore, one time Saint and UNESCO ambassador. Or closer to home, Mother Teresa, a Serbian born to Albanian parents who moved to Calcutta in 1937. But delete the names Diana, Moore and Teresa and insert Pearson, Weatherall and Suggett. For the children of Calcutta in 1976 they were every bit as famous and every bit as inspirational. Life is truly stranger than fiction.

When the players weren't busy laying on hands, some of them ventured a little further. A small gang decided to take a taxi trip around the city. The problem was that Calcutta was not like Rome or London or New York. There weren't a thousand tourist attractions instantly recognisable to the not-well-travelled traveller. They could have gone to the Kali Temple or cultural centre, Tagore House. Then there was the Victoria Memorial at the southern end of The Maidan or St. Paul's Cathedral. And what about the mighty Howrah Bridge, the busiest in the world, arching across The Hooghly in one huge, single 450 metre span. But no, not for our boys. It was perhaps predictable, therefore, that they should ask the wrong question of the driver.

"Hey mate. Can you take us the Black Hole of Calcutta."

The request was met by a silence and look that suggested that this was not something on the normal tourist trail.

"You know. The Black Hole. You must've heard of it.......it is real isn't it?"

"I can't go there sahib. There are many fine places to visit. This is not one of them."

"Oh well.....where do you go for a good time round here?"

The two Charlie's decided they would like to venture out to take in the atmosphere of the covered market near the hotel. There was everything you would expect and more. The garland sellers, the exotic fruit, the lavish fabrics, the sparkling mountains of jewellery, the air thick with spices. The market bounced and swayed and rang out with the bartering calls of traders and buyers. They had their attendant with them, a young lad who would barter for them and take Wrigleys Spearmint gum and a few rupees as payment. But best of all, there was the bloke with the regurgitating act. They stopped and watched with an ever growing crowd, the antics of the man who started by swallowing a jug of water only to bring it straight back up with a triumphant burp. But this was only the entrée. He then proceeded to take a significantly proportioned snake from a sack and feed it, tail first, down his throat. Another confident belch saw the thing slide back out. He tried it again, grinning madly to a captivated but retching audience, only this time the beast got stuck. Eyes bulging and adam's apple popping up and down like a frog in a bag, he stuck his hand half way down his gullet and yanked the reptile from his body before waving it around his head in pure jubilation. Charlie Morrison was sick.

As the players discovered, some people in this intoxicating city didn't go anywhere for a good time. The streets were littered with beggars. On day one of the tour the British High Commissioner had come along to greet the party and warned that they would encounter unpleasant sights but not to feel sorry for them and certainly not to give them money. These situations are not always what they appear to be. Deformed and crippled children hounded the tourists for money.

"No mama. No papa." This was the pathetic devise of an ancient beggar woman with 'borrowed babies' who stared up at the visitors with pleading eyes as she held the infants out towards the passers by. Some of the players were unable to resist the emotional tug and threw coins. Some of the party were visibly upset. It was not unknown for children to be purposely injured in order to present a genuinely disturbing image to the gullible. It was cynical, brutal and not to be encouraged. But it takes a desperate person to cripple a child in order to raise money and begging is not exactly a profession with prospects.

On one occasion, Terry Turnbull and Eric Young, sickened at the thought of tucking into a sumptuous meal at the Oberoi while beggars slept in the streets around the hotel, were moved to action. The food was wonderful, the choice almost endless and the quantities vast. They decided they would smuggle a number of portions outside under their jackets and make their contribution to solving this social problem by feeding some of the beggars that night. They raided the buffet with stealth and purpose and like a couple of seasoned shoplifters, concealed their booty before slipping out of the hotel where they began to distribute the cuisine amongst the hungry. Within seconds they were surrounded by an army of street people who seemed to appear as if from the cracks in the pavement.

"Hold on. We can't feed everyone....Wait a minute...hey, hold on...we've got no more. Sorry...NO MORE...NO MORE...SORRY."

It was getting difficult to be heard let alone understood when suddenly, again as if from nowhere, a posse of policemen descended on the throng wielding batons and battering the beggars with ferocious intent. They were beaten back like a pack of animals and sent scurrying back to their cracks in the pavement. It was quick, it was thorough, it was ruthlessly effective. Eric and Terry were left with mouths agog wondering what on earth they had provoked. They returned with heavy hearts back to the pampered comfort and safety of the Oberoi Grand with an experience that would never leave them.

Eric Young, Jimmy Suggett, Graham Richardson and Terry Turnbull eat roses and drink water at The Oberoi Grand.

The players were able to turn their face from such misery and escape from frenetic pace of the city by attending the Tollygunge Club. The playground of the elite was once the venue for rich frolics in the days of the Raj. Run by retired Englishman, Bob Wright, there was a championship golf course, indoor and outdoor pools, squash and tennis courts, croquet lawns, table tennis, badminton, billiards and a stable of horses to mount at the visitor's convenience. This probably was how the other half lived and it was made possible by a fortuitous connection of Margaret Partridge. Pat's wife was the personal assistant to the Managing Director of the Head Wrightson steel foundary in Thornaby-on-Tees. By a happy coincidence, the company had an office in Calcutta and the MD in Thornaby was the chair of the company in India. He instructed the Indian operation to look after the tourists and ensure they had entertainment whilst in the city. The top man in India,

Kalyan Datta Gupta, was assigned the task of organiser and subsequently arranged access to the Tollgunge Club. Fifteen rupees, the equivalent of around twelve pence, gave each player temporary membership to the club and access all areas. They were treated to top hospitality right down to the finest detail such as servants being made available to dry the feet of the players as they left the pool.

"Hey, make sure you get between the toes."

Not everyone approved of the amount of time that the team was spending at the restorative retreat. It might have been appropriate to the fun-drenched empty heads of the empire but it was no way for a serious football team to be preparing for an important fixture. The very proper and image conscious Dr. Banerjee and manager Jones had one of their regular, heated but quickly forgotten, clashes over the Tollygunge. The players were at the club, talking to some British ex-pats and behaving themselves - even Eric Mac - two days before a game. The doctor had popped in to see them but was not best pleased.

"What are you doing here still? You should be back at the hotel. This is not right."

"Look Dr. Banerjee, I'll come back now if you insist. And I'll pack my bags and go home. I'm not putting up with this. I decide what the players do."

They kissed and made up as they always did – metaphorically that is.

What to eat, where to eat and toilet arrangements are always the great fixations of the British abroad. Bengali cuisine has a leaning towards rice and fish – curried or fried. Sweet specialities include rasgulla, a sweet cream cheese ball flavoured with rose water and misthi, a curd sweetened with jaggery, which is made from palm sap. Despite such attractions, or maybe because of them, fried egg and deep fried chips or steak and chips was popular with the team especially keen to prevent any problems 'down below'. The search was on for plain food that could not be misunderstood. There was no doubt that Margaret Partridge's digestive biscuits were getting a hammering.

The second game of the tour, on the 6th May, was against Mohun Bagan's keenest rivals, East Bengal Athletic Club, champions for the previous six seasons. Eden Gardens was again the venue as ticket holders were 'cordially invited to witness the exhibition football match' between the two teams. In one hundred and one sub-continental degrees of searing sunshine, the team did remarkably well to perform at all let alone come away with a highly creditable 1-1 draw, Darlington midfielder, Eric Young the scorer. The crowd was just as enthusiastic as the first game and almost as large with over 70,000 spectators enduring the stifling conditions. The game had kicked off at 4.00pm and following the final whistle, the players noticed for the first time the dramatic and quite spellbinding spectacle of a huge red sun dropping like a giant orange to be swallowed up by a greedy horizon. But as the players drank in the sight, the huge crowd only had eyes for them. In the case of Crook Town, familiarity was breeding fanaticism. The clamour for tickets did not abate. Players and officials were accosted at every turn to provide tickets for favours. Manager Jones was strolling around a market the day before the game, being treated almost as a new deity, when he came across a jeweller's stall where a particular ring caught his eye.

"Ah. Mr. Jones! You like ring?"

"Yes. Very nice. How much is it? My wife would like it."

"You like ring? You get me ticket for game and is yours."

"Hey, you drive a hard bargain…… It's a deal."

And so with one simple transfer of a match ticket to a market stall holder, Mrs Jones was one snazzy ring to the good. The valuable memento would be presented to her when the team arrived back in England. She still has it. And Bargain Hunters – he might have picked it up 'cheep as chips' but it was a real 'Bobby Dazzler'.

The evening of the second game was when the players decided it was justifiable to let their hair down a bit. There was entertainment in the hotel and the beer was flowing. Calcutta is not unlike any other major world city. There are drinking joints, bars, discos and eateries to suit most tastes. But the hosts had been so meticulous in their planning that almost every night there was an organised drinks reception, meal or entertainment event. This was wonderful for the tourists but occasionally some of the players felt the need to break free from the protocol. When presented with the opportunity, it was difficult to resist.

It was late that evening outside the hotel that a small group of players was approached by a shifty little 'gentleman' offering to take them to a place out of town where they would be able to drink into the night with impunity.

"Hey you. English footballer. You want a good time? I can take you somewhere. You like to drink? See the girls dance?"

The taxi dumped them at a place they would probably rather not have been at that time of night in a strange city.

"Bloody hell. Where are we? What sort of place is this? It looks a bit dodgy."

It had a decidedly back street, seedy joint, watch your back and keep your hands on your wallet sort of feel to it. Once inside, a few of the lads shifted uncomfortably. It was indeed a bit dodgy. It certainly was no Beefeater and they weren't serving chicken in a basket. But the drink was flowing and the dancers were – exotic. At one o'clock in the morning after an extended night of revelry, following a sudden instinctive feeling that they'd be better off not there, the party were back inside the security of a taxi but had still not returned to the hotel. Gordon Jones, sensibly tucked up in bed, was woken by a phone call to his room. It was the local police. They had stopped the taxi taking our heroes across town and accused them of having visited an illegal brothel. Gordon was whisked to the scene to attempt a touch of subtle diplomacy. The problem was the total lack of subtlety on behalf of the policeman. He requested a fistful of rupees to 'turn a blind eye'.

"Turn a blind eye. Turn a blind eye!" Gordon was not on quite the same wavelength and clearly did not know the 'system'.

"I want to see the High Commissioner."

The policeman was unmoved. "These men were at a brothel. You know – young ladies. This is not legal in our city. You will go to prison. What way is this for you to represent your country?"

There were howls of protest. "No we bloody weren't! What's he on about? They were just dancing."

The taxi driver decided it was time to interject a save the situation from getting out of hand.

"Look, You cannot argue with the policeman. He will make life very difficult. You must pay him. It is the best way. Give me the money. I will pass it to him and he will leave you alone. It is the only way. Trust me."

Gordon was fuming but coming to the realisation that a bribe was perhaps the best option. Perhaps the only option. He passed on the cash to the taxi driver who in turn approached the policeman. A short exchange lead to the policeman's mood improving greatly and his waving the taxi on as if nothing had happened. The journey back to the hotel was somewhat subdued.

"Well. Did you go to a brothel?"

"No.... I don't think so.... Did we lads?

"No, no, no. Definitely not....I don't think so anyway."

"I don't want to know."

Back at the hotel, things became clearer. The hotel porter shed light on the incident.

"Ah yes. The police often have an arrangement with the taxi drivers. It's called bribery and corruption. I think your driver got a very good fare tonight."

"Bastard."

The morning of the 7th May provided the early risers with the opportunity to take further advantage of the hospitality of the Tollygunge Club. Their championship golf course was at the disposal of the touring party and several players decided to take advantage of the facilities. They were provided with caddies and, somewhat surprisingly, ball finders. If an errant shot was carved off into the rough or plummeted into a water trap, the ball finder would wade in and search for the ball with the diligence of a prospector in the gold rush. This was not just a means of keeping the play flowing. There was also the small matter of snakes. Obviously it was okay to sacrifice one of the locals but not one of the visiting guests. Manager

Jones and Charlie Morrison, George Potter and Charlie Gott, all had some experience of wielding a golf club and played nine holes before retiring for breakfast under a cooling canopy of trees outside the hotel. Several hackers from the squad followed them round and were equally happy to follow them to breakfast. Terry Turnbull and Eric Young only completed two holes, defeated by their own total inability to play golf. This despite the fact that they had three caddies, one to tee up the ball, one to choose the clubs and one to find the ball. The latter was the most gainfully employed. Anyway, by then it was too hot to continue – and there was always the thought of those snakes.

The non-playing members of the party were entertaining themselves in a variety of ways on a day free from football. Some visited the markets of Calcutta. Some stayed in the shade of the hotel. Others nursed grievances of the gut. Ronnie and Jenny James were treated to a visit to the family home of Dr. Banerjee's sister. The doctor and his wife travelled with them and Charlie Gott to the house in a Calcutta residential area where they were greeted by warm and friendly people who were proud to entertain their guests. Dr. Banerjee's father was also present and had, after all, been a Mohun Bagan player himself in the nineteen thirties and was deeply involved in the tour whose origins could be traced back to his original and continued association with the club. In the most appropriate setting of a Banerjee family home, Ronnie James talked without ceremony to the man whom, along with himself and the doctor, was indirectly responsible for this outrageous tour. Crook Town and Mohun Bagan, past and present, touched for a brief moment in time. A middle class businessman from India's highest caste who had represented his country at football met a working class ex-miner from the north-east of England who had supported his team through good times and bad. The two men were

Pat Partridge and Haradahan Banerjee who is now, aged 94, the oldest living ex-league footballer in India.

joined by a sport-mad doctor who had made the journey from medical school in Calcutta to general practice in Crook. The symbolism was almost certainly lost on the three individuals sharing a drink and a chat. But it is moments like this that form the tangents at which present experience touches the human time-line and creates a little spark of history. Magic.

This was a tour packed with football and match three was scheduled for Saturday 8th May against another of the top teams of the region, Mohammedan Sporting Club. This was the club favoured by the muslim population and the players were exclusively of that religion. However, on this occasion, the Crook team was favoured - by the weather. A heavy downpour in the morning and grey skies throughout the day provided welcome relief from the prevailing conditions on the tour. Eden Gardens hosted yet another enormous crowd that witnessed a much more expansive performance by the visiting team who eventually won 5-1. After fifteen minutes things had not looked good for Crook. Colin Sinclair hit the foot of a post with a penalty and a minute later, Sisir Duha Dastider gave Mohammedan the lead. It was a further penalty in the 33rd minute that offered David Pearson the opportunity to level the scores, which he duly did. This gave heart to the Crook team who proceeded to swamp their opponents in the second half. As our second favourite newspaper, The Sunday Statesman put it:

'After the breather...Crook Town were all over their opponents. Swift, forthright and ruthlessly determined, the British team mounted pressure after pressure and the home team cracked.'

The newspaper reporter was direct in his appraisal of the problem:

'The main reason for Mohammedan Sporting's surprise debacle was the failure of their two midfield players and two link men.........who never went for close tackling.'

I'm sure you are now considering whether or not there is such a thing as 'distant' tackling as opposed to the 'close' type so despised by Mohammedan defenders. Perhaps this is more of a telepathic skill as demonstrated by sixties special agents, The Champions and most of the inhabitants of far-off planets in early editions of Star Trek. At a distance of, say, thirty feet, a defender could 'imagine' an opponent to the ground with a scything thought and simply step in to take the ball away without actually going anywhere near the player. Come to think of it, this is just about the level of contact favoured by FIFA in the modern game. Look out for the next generation of European coaches led by Uri Geller.

Back in the real world, Sinclair, Nattress, Gott and McMordie added four goals in the final twenty minutes to complete a comprehensive rout and manager Jones could be forgiven for looking 'happy at their overwhelming victory.'

May 9th was another rest day. Three matches in five days was taking its toll on the squad who were shedding pounds in fluid loss throughout the games and were thankful for the attentions of the doctor who was always on hand with his 'special' drink and sound medical advice. Not that they were the only ones suffering from the heat. Kit man, Jimmy Gibson had already lost nearly a stone in weight and had been forced to rein in his lime green belt by a full two notches. Many of the touring party were suffering in the plumbing department. Charlie Morrison put it beautifully,

> *"You could be bunged up one day and have the shits the next. There was no pattern to it."*

The doctor carried a cocktail of medicines to encourage or discourage the flow of effluent depending on the immediate requirements of the patient. Before each game Ian Larnach was most particular to ensure that no player's performance would be hindered by doubts over the movement of their bowels.

> *"Right lads, no pulls? No strains? And have you taken your shit stoppers and shit starters?"*

It was to be hoped that everyone was in reasonable digestive order on the 9th since this was the day they had been invited to the British Embassy for cocktails and afternoon tea. It was an honour indeed and an invitation that everyone in full control of their bowels accepted with good grace. Everyone that it, except Eric McMordie. It wasn't that he had anything against The Ambassador or The Crown, it was just that he had a better offer.

> *"I'll not be coming to the embassy. I'm going to the pictures."*

The previous afternoon, after the match, the players had been relaxing in the foyer of the Oberoi Grand when two striking young Indian beauties had entered. Charged with a certain bravado, Eric had challenged his team-mates that he would be able to get a date with one of them. With a lick of the lips he downed his drink and rubbed his hands before heading off across the room to strike up a conversation. As you do.

"Go on my son."

"Get in Eric."

A few minutes later, under the watchful gaze of the rest of the team, he returned with a triumphant smile. The Irish charm had worked a treat. His chosen conquest would be back at seven o'clock prepared for their night out. Unfortunately for Eric, he was not familiar with the protocol of Indian culture in the man/woman department. This was not Middlesbrough town centre on a Friday night. The girl returned punctually at 7.00pm and Eric, dressed to kill and ready for action, was greeted by his chosen one – and her mother. Applauase rang out through the Oberoi Grand as the rest of the team acknowledged their colleague's magnificent 'achievement'.

Our hero returned within the hour with an invitation to a family wedding and the pictures the following day. What better way to see something of the local culture than through a local family. He accepted the kind offer of an afternoon at the movies and was handsomely entertained at the wedding.

Back at the embassy, the rest of the party was having a splendidly civilised afternoon. Jimmy Sugget's hair was to die for after another blow drying from his constant companion, the hair dryer and Terry Turnbull had even turned out in his double-breasted overcoat and trilby. Everyone else respected the occasion by dressing appropriately, politely sipping cocktails, nibbling canapés and then tucking into a huge platter of Ferrero Roches. Oh, Mr. Ambassador did spoil them.

May 10th was the day of the exhibition match against an Indian Football Association select XI. It was a big occasion against what was effectively an Indian national team. However, the day started with an alarming military intervention at 8.00am when two army jeeps screeched to a halt at the entrance to the hotel. The very large, uniformed, cigar smoking Major Mokarjee leaped from his vehicle and stormed into the hotel foyer flanked by several gun-toting henchmen who formed an armed escort.

"Where's Banerjee? I want to see this Dr. Banerjee."

There was genuine trepidation, not to say fear in the air. This did not have the appearance of room service or an Inter Flora delivery. Hotel staff scurried around in a state of blind panic afraid that the visiting doctor was about to be wasted. Dr. Banerjee was in a hotel office sorting out some arrangements for the day when he was interrupted by a hotel receptionist who tried to prepare him for the fact that the Indian army had decided to come and kill him. It was during this hysterical explanation that the door was flung open and in marched the cigar chewing major.

The IFA XI captain shakes hands with Charlie Gott while mascot Anindo Banerjee concentrates on striking a good pose for the camera.

"BANERJEE!....I thought it was you. I read about all this in the newapapers and I said, 'that's him, it's Banerjee.' "

"Mokarjee? It is you isn't it?"

"How long has it been my old friend?"

The two had attended medical school together at RG Kar College. Major Mokarjee was also Dr. Mokarjee and army medic. They probably hadn't spoken for twenty years but made up for it now. There was palpable relief on behalf of the hotel staff. Friends Re-united Indian army style.

The main event of the day was of course the game, which would be played at the home ground of Mohun Bagan before a capacity, forty thousand, crowd. The host club had opened a tent in honour of their guests and the day was liberally sprinkled with speeches by the Indian hosts and words of appreciation by the English visitors. The non-playing members of the touring party were treated with the utmost courtesy and respect and afforded hospitality to match. This culminated in a presentation after the game at which every member of the party was given a solid silver dish and spoon as a memento of the occasion. The tourists were almost overwhelmed by the generosity of their hosts. Everyone that is, except Terry Turnbull. Before the presentation of gifts the Select XI manager had been asked to say a few words. As the assembled visitors and dignitaries gathered in the shade of the Mohun Bagan tent, the team manager gave a very personal view of what he had seen.

> *"I do not like this style of football. We are very disappointed. The ball is in the air far too much. It should be called headball not football. This not how we in India prefer to play the game. And (wagging a finger disparagingly towards the larger than life visiting centre forward) this 'Terrybull' – we don't like this type of player. This 'Terrybull' is not good player."*

Now 'Big T' was a bruiser no doubt. But just because you're big and hairy doesn't mean you have no feelings. Terry was a bit deflated by this singular attack. There was also a whiff of home town embarrassment in the air as heads shook shamefully and faces reddened. It fell to Gordon Jones to step in and respond as the opposing manager. He proceeded to give a treatise on the merits of the British style of football evoking memories of Tommy Lawton to demonstrate the need for a strong, direct and aggressive front man, of which type Terry was a classic. The speech did wonders for 'Big T' and pricked the bubble of tension caused by the indiscreet home manager. The assembled guests relaxed visibly back into their seats, diplomatic crisis averted.

Before the game both teams had been introduced to the IFA president, Mr. Gouri Mitter and two 'well-known sports personalities in the yesteryears', Chhoney Mazumder and Bagh Shome, who were warmly welcomed by the crowd and would also be two of the retired players to benefit financially from the money raised by the match.

The IFA XI lined up 4-2-4:

T. Bose

S. Karmakar   S. Battacharjee   S. Ghosh   Dilip Sarkar

S. Choudhury   G. Sarkar

Ulganathan   S. Bhowmick   Habib   Latifuddin

Crook Town lined up 4-4-2:

G. Richardson

B. Agar   S. Bell   G. Potter   C. Nattress

P. Brown   C. Morrison   P. Weatherall   C. Gott

J. Suggett   D. Pearson

Substitute appearances: Horner, McMordie, Turnbull, Young, Sinclair

On the field of play, the generosity of the host organisers was matched only by that of the Crook players who squandered chance after chance during a match that didn't really catch light until after the break. Indian international forward, Habib, scored the Select XI goal with a deft lob over the onrushing Richardson early in the second half and for once, our friends at The 'Patrika' were not singing the praises of the Crook 'keeper.

> *'But in all fairness to the brilliant piece of scoring zeal, it must also be admitted that the visiting custodian, Richardson, left his charge unnecessarily without assessing the flight of Sarkar's long lob and anticipating Habib's stance in right perspective.'*

But it wasn't all Graham's fault. The true problem was the lack of accuracy in front of goal. The 'Patrika', again;

> *'It was a cool and pleasant afternoon, the sun hiding behind a thick veil of clouds and a gentle south wind blowing down the field. All to the liking of the Albions. And the way they began pounding the home citadel from the very start one expected another fluent win for the visitors. Exhibiting better speed, stamina and cohesion, Crook Town overshadowed the IFA XI in no uncertain manner. Improving with every outing, they revealed some of the basic qualities of the modern European footballer. Their hard tackling, neat inter-passing and swift inter-change of positions were a real treat for the jam-packed stands. But what they really lacked and paid for dearly, was their poor finish.'*

Crook must have wasted a dozen scoring chances including a missed penalty by George Potter, Hartlepool's Scottish full-back. But they also suffered misfortune as the lovely 'Patrika' noted;

> *'Dame luck also eluded them on the day for twice in the first half the woodwork came to the rescue of the IFA XI.'*

At the final whistle, Ronnie James turned to wife, Jenny to remind her of an incident at the team hotel on the second day of their visit. An Indian holy man cum philosopher was sitting cross-legged on the floor in a large bay window in the reception. He beckoned Ronnie over to him and gave his verdict on the outcome of the tour.

> *"I have good news for you. You will have a very successful tour – but you will lose one game. One of your players will do a very silly thing."*

George Potter had missed his penalty in spectacular fashion. Some say they've never seen a ball hit so high over a cross bar. A very silly thing indeed. The cross-legged clairvoyant was spot on though.

Dame luck also eluded Gordon Jones that day. He missed the match because of a dose of something nasty in the pants region. He took ill after lunch and was immediately confined to barracks. Maybe it was lunch or perhaps The Ambassador's canapés were taking their revenge. Nevertheless, it was Billy Horner and Ian Larnach that oversaw proceedings and picked the team. Luckily, whatever the source of the manager's affliction, it was mercifully short-lived. After spending a few hours in sick bay, Gordon was miraculously on the mend. But not before Peter Weatherall and David Pearson had raised his blood pressure a few notches. They dashed back from the game to give their stricken manager the bad news.

> *"Hey, Gordon. There's hell on back there. We were crap. Got stuffed five nil. Tackles flying everywhere. Charlie lost it and clouted Pat Partridge. He had to be carried off..."*

They could contain it no longer and dissolved into fits of laughter. The rapidly healing manager was fit enough to chase them down the corridor.

Fully recovered, Gordon joined Eric Mac and Billy for a quiet drink in a local bar and they were pretty impressed by the standard of the ale. However, as Eric returned from the bar with his round he stopped in his tracks, stared over Billy's shoulder and – now let me stop you at this point to allow you to recall the moment in the film 'Jaws' when the inspector of police accompanying Quint to go shark fishing on his old boat, drops his cigarette from his mouth and retreats in shock to the cabin. He's just seen the monster rise from the water to take the bait and bare his teeth to the cinema audience for the first time and he utters the immortal words, "You're gonna need a bigger boat."

Eric had just seen a huge rat sitting bolt upright at the foot of a partition behind the table with a nonchalance that would have only been exceeded had it folded it's arms and tapped it's feet. His gaze never left the rat as he uttered what should become the immortal words, "Next time you go to the bar, you'd better get your friend a drink."

The three brave soldiers downed their drinks in one and left the bar quicker than their furry friend up a drain pipe. Meanwhile, Terry and Charlie Morrison were out for a stroll around town, hoping to catch a few light ales before retiring, exhausted to the hotel. As ever there was a constant stream of attention from the local beggars and street folk anxious to relieve the visitors of a few rupees. However, on this occasion the beggar in chief was a tall, quite athletic looking lad, with the dreadful handicap of surviving on the street with only one arm and one leg. When he persisted in his efforts, the players felt secure in the knowledge that at least here was one beggar who wasn't going to follow them around. They didn't account for the possibility that his one leg was as good as two on most men. After shunning his advances and heading off down the street, they were shocked to hear this singular 'thud-thud' sound behind them and spun around to see our friend bounding down the road like a demented, human pogo stick. To say that he was 'fleet of foot' would be a terrible pun but terribly accurate. Perhaps still in a state of shock or maybe genuinely impressed at his persistence – and balance – they caved in for once and gave him a tip.

Day nine of the Indian adventure was drawing to a close. The tour was more than anyone had dared to dream about back in the Millfield Ground clubhouse all those months ago when Dr. Banerjee was teased about the possibility of visiting India. Performances and results had been highly creditable and the response from the Indian public quite phenomenal. Crook had played the country's three best and most important club teams without losing and had received a welcome from the Indian establishment that wouldn't have disgraced the English national team. After only four of the scheduled fixtures, over a quarter of a million people had seen them play. Surely, it couldn't get any better than this.

The Moon over Everest

News of the Crook tour was spreading throughout India and particularly the state of West Bengal. So much so, that the state government intervened to 'suggest' an additional fixture. It would be a great honour if the tourists would be their guests for a diversionary trip to Darjeeling where they could play an exhibition match for the local people against Mohun Bagan. All expenses would be paid, of course. Persuasion was not required. Should they go? Is the pope a catholic?

Our favourite newspaper, The 'Patrika', summed up the mood of the nation in a piece filed from the Darjeeling office on May 10th.

> *'The whole of Darjeeling district, nay, the entire stretch of the mountain region in this part, extended up to Sikim and Bhutan, is gripped with an unprecedented enthusiasm for the exhibition football match between Crook Town club from England and Calcutta's famous team, Mohun Bagan.....Rains every night have kept the temperature low and rendered the North Point Ground suitable for the visiting team's football....The All India Radio will broadcast a running commentary of the play in Nepali and Bengali...'*

The fixture was agreed at an early stage in the tour and scheduled for Wednesday 12th May at 2.30pm. The party was looking forward to a change of environment and a change of temperature. They were told that Darjeeling would offer some relief because of its altitude. This was, after all, the West Bengal Hills, effectively the foothills of The Himalayas, which is quite famous for being high up and a bit chilly. It's equally famous for being the home of one of the first two men to stand on the top of the world. Sherpa, Tenzing Norgay lived in the former British army hill station until his death in 1986. He was the director of the Himalayan Mountaineering Institute for many years, earning his living from the hills that made him famous, always in sight of the scene of his historic achievement. The players of Crook Town had been invited to this magical, almost mystical place. It was too good an opportunity to miss.

On the morning of the 11th May, the touring party completed their ablutions, breakfasted in the usual fine fashion and powdered their collective nose. They packed a bag and prepared for the journey to Calcutta airport, known locally as Dum Dum after the dum dum barracks where the explosive and devastating bullet of the same name was manufactured, only to be banned after the Boer war. They gathered in the hotel lobby, waiting for the taxis that would pick their way to Dum Dum. As they were about to check out for a couple of nights, a member of the hotel staff decided it was time to settle the drinks bill. This is the tab that manager Jones had insisted upon after witnessing 100,000 paying fans at the first game of the tour. The bill was running at a figure approximating to £1000 but payment was not what Gordon had intended when he demanded a tab. Just as he was beginning to challenge the bill, chairman, Wilf Collingwood, who was ambling down the stairs to the lobby, overheard the exchange. Gordon glanced up to see a panic-stricken Wilf descending one of the grandest staircases in Calcutta, his trousers tied with a length of string and a face that betrayed a head filled with dreadful consequences.

"Bloody hell. A thousand pounds. We can't afford a thousand pounds. Who the bloody hell has had a thousand pounds worth of drinks?"

Ronnie James, suddenly catching the panic like a Mexican wave became equally apoplectic.

"A thousand pounds. Oh, my God....that's it. We're buggered."

He and Wilf flapped around like a pair of knickers on a washing line in a force nine gale. But the negotiations continued.

"Mr. Jones, can I ask you to settle the bill please?"

"No, no. I think you must be mistaken, bonny lad. We are not expecting to pay for drinks."

"Oh, no, Mr. Jones....you must pay."

"We won't be paying for the drinks."

"I'm sorry, Mr. Jones...it is the policy of the hotel...I must insist..."

"All right. If we pay for these drinks, we don't go to Darjeeling. Now then, I suggest you go back there and telephone the West Bengal Government and let them know that we're not coming. See how that goes down, eh?"

A look of horror spread across the face of the young Oberoi Grand man. Could he really be responsible for the collapse of the great India tour? The public of India would lynch him. He disappeared and returned after a period of five minutes, relieved and smiling and with head held high in triumph, exclaimed,

"Mr. Jones....your bill has been paid."

"Good lad. I knew you'd understand."

"Sahib."

Wilf and Ronnie pulled themselves together, the party headed for the taxis and they bade a temporary farewell to the Oberoi Grand as they were transported to Calcutta airport amid cheering crowds on the city streets. Even their movements to and from the hotel were followed fanatically by the Indian supporters.

The nearest airport to Darjeeling was Bagdogra, just over fifty miles due south of the town. The twin propeller, wing flapper was not quite the state of the art technology that had brought them the India on the Jumbo Jet. However, on this occasion, the pain would only last for one and a half hours for the 'fly-shy' Terry Turnbull before they were transferred to a small fleet of rickety old buses for the final leg of the journey. On this occasion, the party was joined by players and officials from Mohun Bagan, their opponents for the exhibition match. They too were guests of the government. They too were anticipating a cool break from the furnace that was Calcutta. By now, the players getting to know each other quite well so the flight was convivial and friendly.

The road to Darjeeling followed the same route as the railway line from Siliguri and New Jalpaiguri. Within fifty miles, they would climb over three thousand feet to the their destination above the clouds at seven thousand feet. The buses threaded their way through the hills, a gradual but constant ascent, crossing the railway or parallel to it at several points where they were able to wave to the packed and bulging carriages that seemed to contain a whole nation of smiling, happy travellers, in some cases, hanging from the sides of the train. The mechanical beast of burden would have been a living nightmare for the Durham County Council health and safety officer had he seen it. Which, of course he didn't because he wasn't there. Thank God.

They passed through Kurseong, smaller, peaceful and less commercial than Darjeeling and blessed with mountain walks and the prolific white orchid after which it was named. Lush, green hills, mountain forests, tumbling streams and tufts of cloud were all seemingly within touching distance as the convoy passed through Ghoom and clawed its way up into Darjeeling, sprawling over a west-facing ridge and spilling carelessly down the hillside. The hills that surrounded the town carried over eighty tea gardens, producing twenty five percent of the country's total crop and employing forty thousand people from the surrounding area. This was possibly the most beautiful place in the world and yes, there really is an awful lot of tea in Darjeeling.

On entering 'The Place of the Thunderbolt' through a complex network of roads and footpaths it was clear that they were expected. "WELCOME THE CROOKS TOWN". The banner was strung across the road in honour of the team. What a pity that one misplaced 's' made it sound like a homecoming for a bunch of convicts fresh from a twenty year stretch. Nevertheless, the sentiments were typical of the hospitality of the Indian people who also came out in force to line the streets of their mountain paradise by way of a welcome. Home for the next two nights was the Himalayan Hotel, a sixteen room, former family home of British diplomat David MacDonald, who was British political officer in Sikkim, India's most northerly province, in the early twentieth century. After its conversion to a hotel it was home to a number of Everest expeditions including Mallory and Irving in the 1920s. Hillary and Tenzing were regular guests. The place dripped with history. So much so that some of the players thought it haunted, certainly spooky. Each room had a coal fire and 'boasted' hot and cold running water.

Unfortunately, there was a water shortage at the time of the Crook visit and they were asked to expect the water to be available only at certain times. This was a fact of life in the mountain community where services could never be taken for granted because of the effects of severe weather. The trouble was, Pat Partridge had a game to referee and water shortages were not part of his preparations.

"Hold on a minute. I'm afraid I can't referee without a bath."

"I'm sorry, sahib. It is the way in Darjeeling. We sometimes have problems."

"Whenever I exercise, I must have a bath afterwards. It's part of my

routine. It's part of my preparation for the next game. Oh, no. I can't carry on without a bath."

The hotel management was on to the case immediately. Aware that Pat was performing in every match for ninety minutes and equally aware that, as guests of the government, it wouldn't be a good idea to upset the tourists, they came back to the Partridge room with firm assurances.

"Mr. Partridge, you will have your bath. It has been arranged."

"Ah, excellent. But how can you be sure...."

" It has been arranged. You need not fear. Enjoy your bath Mr. Partridge."

Pat was left pondering how it had been arranged. Had some poor townsfolk been coerced to bring water to the hotel in buckets then made to stoke up boilers with their broken furniture and forced to carry jugs of hot water to his room? Or was he getting carried away? Like good managers, they sorted it. It's what managers do. Say no more.

The party settled into the hotel. It was friendly and accommodating. The rooms were spacious and comfortable and there were servants at the beck and call of every person. The pace of life dropped suddenly and dramatically compared to the frenzy of Calcutta. It was no wonder that this was a favourite holiday destination for Indian big city dwellers. Though cooler than Calcutta, it was still humid and clothes would often be dampened when walking out. In Darjeeling you can literally stroll through the clouds. This was a place of romance and mystique and of views of the highest and most dramatic mountain range in the world. Lhotse, Makalu, Kanchenjunga and Everest formed a humbling skyline. Peace had descended on the tour. After the welcome banners and the greetings, they were able to walk about the town free from the all-consuming attentions of fans. Perhaps this was because now, in the high season, many of the people were tourists, here for the same peace and tranquillity or for one of the organised treks to the Himalayan mountains. Either way, for the first time on the tour, the players were able to take in some of the atmosphere of their host country at their own pace, in their own time.

Once again, it was agreed that training would be pointless after the long journey and in the stifling humidity. Consequently, no-one saw the pitch

Dressed for dinner at the Governor of West Bengal's residence. A truly spectacular array of ties.

before the actual game the following day. It meant that the players could be tourists for the rest of the day before dining in the evening with representatives of the West Bengali government at Governor Dias' residence. Having been royally entertained, they retired to their rooms that night at peace with the world. As Pat Partridge prepared for bed, he stepped onto the balcony and taking a breath of cool air, stared into a cloudless sky.

"Margaret. Come and look at this."

"What's wrong?"

"Look at that. Can you believe we're standing here looking at the moon over Everest?"

Everyone with a room facing to the north-west was drinking in the same astonishing view of a streaked, silver moon hovering above the top of the world. This was a once-in-a-lifetime moment. Just stand for a moment and take it in......

The big game was to be played on the afternoon of Wednesday the 12th of

May. Both Mohun Bagan and Crook players spent a restful morning strolling around the town doing some sight seeing and shopping. Mainly centred in the Chowrasta district, the typical souvenir shops were filled with objects derived from the Tibetan mountain culture that so influences Darjeeling. Thangkas, the rectangular Tibetan religious cloth paintings, brass statues, wood carvings and carpets were in abundance. Then there were the magnificent prints of Kanchenjunga and tea, tea, tea and more tea. Chowk Bazaar, the air redolent with spices and incense was fascinating and gloriously tacky.

Sightseeing over, the teams returned to the hotel where they were to change for the game before being transported to the venue an hour before the game. The match was to be played at a local school, North Point, which didn't have permanent changing rooms but had erected some temporary facilities for the teams to use at halftime and full time. What greeted them as they approached the ground was unlike anything either team had ever encountered. After disembarking with their kit bags, they were ushered through a gathering crowd and down a steep hillside. Thousands of people were clinging to the slopes leading down to a plateau that appeared to be cut out of the mountain. Applause rang around the hillside as the spectators realised that this was the 'famous' Crook team. The teams had actually been brought into the ground through the crowd then taken around the pitch to the changing accommodation at the far end. The playing field was surrounded on three sides by the natural mountain terraces and on the fourth by a sheer drop down to the tea plantations. Only a twenty-feet-high mesh fence stood between a frisky sliding tackle and a long journey south on the backside. Standing at the changing room door, the teams would look forward and right to see a mass of Indian football fanatics growing out of the wooded slopes like forty thousand white orchids from Kurseong. To the left they would see a ball boy's worst nightmare.

The playing surface itself was something new to both teams. Not a blade of grass could be seen. The match would be played out on a creamy, compressed sand and clay concoction. And in an act typical of the Indian welcome, the club motifs of Mohun Bagan and Crook Town had been painted in meticulous detail onto the centre of the pitch. The school had erected the obligatory tent for hospitality and special guests that included representatives from the West Bengal government, including The Governor and of course, the two visiting teams. All were specially presented with Darjeeling silk scarves. The rest of the crowd was made up of locals -

businesses had closed at noon so employees could attend the match - school children and astonishingly, hundreds of people who had travelled for days to see the game. West Bengal and the surrounding mountain people had seen nothing like it. If the game was history in the making for Crook, it was just as important to Darjeeling.

Gordon Jones, Billy Horner and trainer, Ian Larnach prepared the team in the usual way with all squad members scheduled to appear in the game and once again, the teams were greeted by a phenomenal ovation that rang around the mountain shelf on which they found themselves. After the presentation to the dignitaries the game followed the same predictable pattern of the previous encounters. Nice one-touch stuff by the Indians and a bit of the old route one by Crook. Although, even in this, the fifth game of the tour, there was still enough bite on the pitch to keep things interesting. Nevertheless, as half time arrived, the game was still scoreless. The consolation for the players was that there is no more appropriate place on earth to have a half time cup of tea.

After being suitably rested and refreshed, referee Pat Partridge rang the specially provided half time bell to call out the two teams. However, Eric McMordie had sneaked out slightly early take in the view and met Pat on the way back in.

"Can't go out now, Pat"

"What do you mean, can't?"

"If I was you, I'd go back in and get another cup of tea. There's a steamroller on the pitch."

Pat took a look outside and sure enough, there was an old roller steaming and trundling up and down the pitch flattening out the surface for the second half.

"Steamroller stopped play lads. Might as well grab another cuppa."

After spending ten minutes watching an impromptu steam rally, the players returned to the action to see out a 1-1 draw in true exhibition fashion, the two goals, by Habib and Turnbull, being greeted with equal delight by a totally impartial crowd. The ball never once carried the mesh fence. The ball boys went home happy.

The players left the field to yet another great ovation. They waved to the crowd and saluted their hosts in an orgy of mutual appreciation and returned, exhausted to the temporary dressing room where they wondered out loud if anything more spectacular could happen on this extraordinary tour. Scrubbed up and changed, they grabbed their bags to head back out, walk back around the field and climb the steps by which they had entered the arena through cheering fans three hours earlier. Only now, as they stood at the changing pavilion door, there was no crowd. There were only a few officials and ground staff. There was no stadium, just a hillside. A plain and simple hillside with grass, trees and a few rocks. Any infrastructure they had assumed to be beneath the backsides of the spectators had been imagined. Forty thousand Indian tourists and football fans had vanished leaving everything as nature had intended. Had they really played a football match here?

Steam roller stopped play – Darjeeling.

Back at the hotel it was an evening of relaxation and self-made entertainment. No official banquets to attend. No formal visits. The players of both teams could walk around town, have a meal and have a drink and be relatively free from well-wishers and fans. Pat Partridge had his ritual post exercise bath – another family without furniture as the boilers were stoked to heat his water and he was exposed to the usual gentle ref bating that was to be expected amongst a squad of players over whom he had just officiated.

"Bloody hell Pat, call yerself a FIFA ref."

"You don't even know when someone's gone over the top. He nearly broke my bloody leg."

"Is there a pea in that whistle, Pat?"

The atmosphere was genial. The party was in good humour and Darjeeling was a kind of paradise. This felt like as good as it gets.

The following morning, it was time to check out of the Himalayan Hotel and head back to Calcutta. The West Bengal government officials were there to see them off as were yet more cheering and adoring fans and hotel staff. Back in the rickety bus convoy they retraced their journey back down the road alongside the railway, turning to see the mountain retreat disappearing behind them and saying a lump–in-the-throat goodbye to Everest and Kanchenjunga. However, silent regrets about leaving this magical world were shattered by a simple and basic request.

"Stop the bus. I need the loo."

Groans all round.

"Come on. I'm desperate."

The bus duly stopped at the side of the road.

"Hurry up Pat. Get a move on."

"All right. All right. Just give me a few minutes."

"A few minutes to have a slash. What have you been drinking?"

"I don't want a slash."

It had to be Pat. Another excuse for a bout of good natured ref bating. As he disappeared out of site down the hill, several players were seen to be hanging out of the bus windows and heard to be shouting,

"Hey Pat, you're shit, you."

"That's shite that is Pat."

"We know what you're doing."

Hoots of laughter and buckets of fun replaced the feelings of loss at leaving Darjeeling. Normality returned to the party courtesy of an international referee taking a dump in the bushes.

A Paine for the President

On the night of the 14th May, the big rains came. The heavens cracked open and poured water on the world in an Old Testament kind of way. Little men with beards were heard hammering planks together to build boats while their wives collected two chickens, two cockroaches and two Bengal tigers just in case they had to re-populate the planet with animals in a post-diluvial safari park. The road outside the Oberoi Grand was a river. Duckboards were seen floating off down the road and cars struggled against the tide like boats tied loosely to their moorings. All in all, it was not a good night to leave the washing out on the line.

The big problem was that the 15th May was the date of the tour finale, a match against the Chief Minister's X1, the chief minister being the country's president. When it was still raining in the morning and the roads were still awash with water, it seemed an open and shut case – the game's off. After breakfast, Mohun Bagan organising secretary, Dhiren Dey approached Pat Partidge with a request to do a pitch inspection.

"Mr. Partridge. I think you will need to inspect the pitch to be sure the game can proceed."

"Inspect the pitch! Look at it out there. There's still a foot of water on the road. It's water polo conditions. We'll never get a game today."

"I think you should go to inspect the pitch. There is always a chance. You may be surprised."

"Surprised!....Surprised!.....Look at it man!"

" I have a driver waiting for you outside, Mr. Partridge."

"All right. But it'll take a miracle."

"Have faith Mr. Partridge."

Leaving nothing to chance, Dhiren Dey had arranged the superintendent of police to drive Pat to Eden Gardens. They crawled through mini lakes and slow moving rivers in the Calcutta streets with Pat mumbling all the way about the utter madness of it all and the superintendent equally adamant that the show must go on. When they arrived at Eden Gardens neither opinion had altered. They were forced to wade out to the centre of the playing surface through four inches of rain water on the outfield. The terraces were swimming and the enclosures were just as bad. Miraculously, however, just as had been predicted, the actual football pitch had cleared of water and whilst damp and heavy, was clearly draining and drying quickly.

"Blimey, I don't believe it."

"It drains well, Mr. Partridge....So the match is on then?"

"Now hold on a minute. What about the rest of the field? And what about the spectators? That terrace is a dam hazard."

"Forget about such diversions Mr. Partridge. You must concentrate on the pitch."

The Indian President (centre with shades) surrounded by players from Crook, the the Chief Ministers' XI plus the rest of the Crook entourage before the last game of the tour.

"Well... I suppose....well the pitch is okay I suppose."

"Excellent, Mr. Partridge. You have made many people very happy. The game is on!"

It seemed impossible when he left the hotel but the pitch was playable and at the rate the water was draining away, it was just feasible that the rest of the field and terraces could clear as well.

While the inspection was taking place, Ronnie James and Gordon Jones were making a crucial visit to Calcutta airport. The 9.00am arrival from Bombay was carrying precious cargo, the centre-piece for the final game of the tour, the World Cup star that the Indian authorities had craved. Terry Paine, veteran of 815 League matches and nineteen England caps, including one in the World Cup finals in 1966, was knackered but he was there. Coming towards the end of a career that began in 1956 and spent almost entirely at Southampton, Terry had played his final two seasons at Hereford United, guiding them to promotion to the second division just a few short days before flying out to India. It had been hoped that he would make it for more than one game but Hereford's continued progress in the Welsh FA Cup meant his departure was delayed. The tired and jet-lagged star was taken immediately to the Oberoi Grand where he was able to put his head down and get some sleep before the 3.00pm kick-off. They knew that the game was another sell-out and there was a good chance the president himself could be in attendance. It was vital that Terry Paine was out there shaking hands with the captain of the Chief Minister's X1. It was equally vital that he didn't fall asleep on his feet in front of a hundred thousand expectant fans.

Another cause for concern was the referee. Pat Partridge was pissed off. Forced to undertake a pitch inspection in a pair of waders and almost brow beaten into agreeing the pitch was playable, the man was physically drained. As the only person on the tour, barring goalkeeper, Graham Richardson, who had spent the full ninety minutes of every match on the field of play, he was exhausted. At ten o'clock the previous morning, one of the Indian tour organisers had visited Pat to inform him that he would be refereeing the last game.

"No I'm bloody not!"

"Ah, yes, I see Mr. Partridge...a joke."

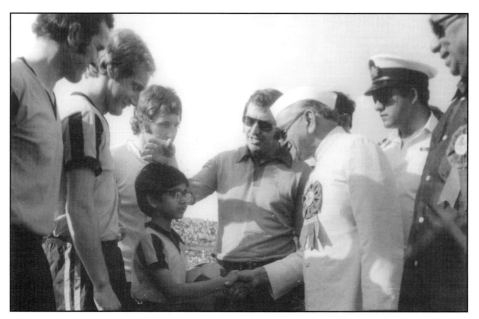

Terry Paine, Charlie Gott and Billy Horner look on as Anindo Banerjee is presented to the Indian President by Gordon Jones.

"No joke. I've had it. My legs are like lead. I can't perform like this. I prepare professionally for my games and this is not proper preparation. You've got FIFA refs running the line. One of them can do it."

The official left convinced this was just a momentary lapse of reason on Pat's part. Pat was left fuming, convinced that he was being taken for granted. This would not be the end of the matter. On the match day a seriously miffed referee decided to put his foot down. He was not going to officiate. The Indian linesmen were all recognised FIFA officials. One of them could do it. But for some reason the Indian hosts were in a blind panic at the thought of one of their own carrying the whistle. Pat left the hotel for Eden Gardens with a long easy stride, a relaxed, even carefree air and two hands swinging free. He had no bag, therefore no gear, therefore no intention of refereeing. Officials of both parties watched him leave with mouths agog, chins on chests and a mounting realisation that a crisis had just left the building. The whispers hissed around the lobby, the nudges and nods multiplied.

"He's flipped...He's lost his grip."

"The sun's got to him."

"He can't walk out now. What the hell are we going to do?"

"Not the last match, surely. This is the big one. He can't just leave us in it."

The players gathered in the foyer to set off for Eden Gardens for the last time. The regular morning press call had been completed, their taxis awaited and the crowds gathered. But there was a significant, slightly sinister addition to the routine. Armed guards had appeared in the hotel corridors and when the team left the Oberoi Grand, the streets had been cleared of vehicles and the Indian army lined the route to the stadium. The journey had been reduced to ten minutes courtesy of an armed escort. This was really the only way to travel in Calcutta. Thousands of ticketless fans, curious onlookers and heavily restrained oxen viewed the convoy through the massed ranks. This was the type of treatment usually reserved for royalty or the highest officials of the Indian government but now Crook Town had been added to that exalted list.

When they arrived at the stadium, yet again, it was full to overflowing. And this time there were two added ingredients for the fans. Firstly, Terry Paine and secondly their own president. It had been confirmed that Sri Fakhruddin Ali Ahmed would indeed be in attendance. Or as the never less than ostentatious tickets put it, 'The President of India will grace the occasion with his presence'. Perhaps the reason for the heavy armour? In any case, the final game had an air of something special about it. Unfortunately, with twenty minutes to go before kick-off, there was also an air of desperation because no-one was quite sure who would be wielding the whistle. In the officials' dressing room five Indian referees sat nervously awaiting the decision on which of them would be chosen to run the line. Pat Partridge, still in no mood for compromise, sat down beside them. The organisers were red-faced with panic and confusion. Blood pressure was rising to danger levels. Heads would roll, after all this was the game to raise money for the President's charity. This was not the time for cock-ups. However, what nobody had noticed as Pat left the hotel was that Margaret had followed on behind with his kit bag. She'd also slipped into Eden Gardens with the very same bag while the organisers were busy being apoplectic.

As kick-off grew dangerously close, a whole range of people were reaching for the bicycle clips as sphincter control lapsed with every passing second. When the hysteria reached comic proportions and Pat feared someone might actually explode, he stepped forward.

"All right, all right, I'll do it."

" Oh, Mr. Partridge, this is excellent news. Thank you, thank you."

A great weight was lifted from proceedings and the relief so evident that you could smell it. Humility reigned amongst the hosts. Pat had made his protest and had his fun but he always knew he would relent

"Listen...we don't treat referees like this in England. I hope you've learned your lesson. Right...I'll get my kit."

Everything was set for the grand finale. The two teams lined up side by side to walk onto the pitch and receive the acclaim of the crowd. Crook were in the now familiar black and gold, the Chief Minister's XI in all white. But before the grand entrance a whirring, hammering engine noise was

Wilf Collingwood, Jayasree and Dr. Banerjee meet the Indian president at Eden Gardens.

heard high above the city and clearly getting closer to the stadium. As the clattering sound grew ever louder it became clear that a helicopter was coming in to land. It was coming in to land right in the centre of the field. One hundred thousand heads turned to the sky and watched in stunned amazement as the craft descended onto the pitch which should have been welcoming the players. The rotor blades slowed and flopped to a standstill allowing the occupants to disembark. It was then announced that the President of India, Fakhruddin Ali Ahmed, had indeed arrived. And he'd arrived in some style. The crowd gave respectful applause to their leader as he milked the moment in that special, politicians' way and it was then that the two teams were introduced to the fans. They entered the arena to a familiar but no less remarkable ovation and lined up to be introduced to the leader of the host nation. However, there was one final introduction. Terry Paine, was given the PA treatment and hailed as the England World Cup star that he was. Any lingering fears that the disappointment of Bobby Charlton's non-appearance would over-shadow Terry's arrival were instantly quashed by a reception to remember. He ran, waving onto the field to a rapturous and appreciative ovation. Bobby might not be there but Terry had made the effort and the Indian public was grateful.

Captain for the day, World Cup star Terry Paine, exchanges pennants with the captain of the Chief Ministers' XI before the final mach of the India Tour.

All of the key participants were then lined up for the world's biggest team photo. Mohun Bagan players and officials, Crook Town players and officials, other assembled dignitaries and tour organisers, members of the touring party and mascot, Anindo Banerjee seated right in front of the president. Dr. Banerjee was proudly positioned behind the president having successfully brought the small time football team from his adopted English town to play in his home country's most prestigious venue before its highest citizen. Twelve months ago this moment would have seemed inconceivable. The experience of the whole tour would have seemed inconceivable. But here, with the president of India, in front of one hundred thousand people, a dream had been realised. What had started out as a joke had really happened. What no other football team in the world had achieved, Crook Town had. Displaying his pride on a team photograph was the least that the doctor should be allowed.

Terry Paine assumed the role of captain for the day, exchanging club pennants with the Mohun Bagan top man at the toss, flanked by the regular captain, Charlie Gott and mascot, Anindo. But this was not before one last bouquet throwing exhibition by the two teams who whipped the crowd into a frenzy by flinging flowers at the spectators. It was a joyous

Action versus the Chief Ministers' XI at Eden Gardens. I wonder how much Boroline paid for that advert?

atmosphere and one that demanded a last hurrah from the tourists. Knackered Pat Partridge summoned up enough energy to blow the whistle and start the match then proceeded to officiate heroically after his protest. Crook battled like giants against eleven fresh men, their own tired legs, heat and humidity and were eventually rewarded with a highly creditable 1-1 draw. The Chief Minister's XI was, to all intents and purposes, a national team and Crook's pride had carried them through to a final, honourable draw thanks to one last goal from Colin Sinclair. Once again, target man Terry Turnbull was a major influence and a focal point of the visitors' tactics. His reputation enhanced by the tour, Terry would be signed by Hartlepool United the following season and make his League debut shortly before his thirty first birthday.

For Terry Paine it was a great experience, a great reception but one game too far in a long season for a thirty-seven year old veteran with severe jet lag and a Welsh Cup Final in his legs. The newspaper reports the next day were not kind to him suggesting that it would have been hard to spot the World Cup star had he not been announced to the crowd before the game.

> *'If we had not known who the international player was we would never have picked him out.'*
> **Our friends at The 'Patrika'. Usually entertaining but this time, talking bollocks.**

But even if the hacks were unreasonable, the public was not and he was treated as an honoured guest. The Crook players were proud to have appeared alongside him though with a lightening schedule that was based around flying in, playing a game, getting some sleep and flying home, it was no surprise that none was able to really get to know him. Nevertheless, when the game ended, there was much slapping of backs, swapping of shirts, hugging, shaking of hands, waving to a rapturous crowd – and relief that the Crook Town bodies had survived a ground breaking, quite extraordinary but utterly exhausting tour. They had played six competitive matches in twelve days in temperatures often in excess of one hundred degrees Fahrenheit and humidity that seemed to wrap around like a big soggy blanket. They had played a nation's top teams and two top representative XIs and emerged with their heads held high and their reputation as footballers enhanced.

As the players retired to the dressing room, the cheers of the crowd still ringing in their ears, spent limbs flopping down on the benches, it began to dawn on them that the great adventure was coming to an end. The only logical next step was to have a few beers to round off a memorable day. They left Eden Gardens for the last time through yet more fanatical crowds desperate to get a closer look at the departing heroes or even a treasured autograph, before finally being ferried by taxi through the admiring and persistent gathering back to the hotel. Another reception had been arranged for the tour party, this time to express the mutual thanks and appreciation that were heart felt and sincere and for Mohun Bagan to present Crook town with a wonderful trophy as a memento of this magical tour.

The next major sporting occasion for the spectators at the Ranji Stadium, Eden Gardens, would be the test match, starting on New Year's Day 1977, which formed part of England's winter tour of India in 1976-77. The tourists, including Knott, Greig, Amiss, Bearley, Willis and Underwood were accommodated at The Oberoi Grand. It's where all the best people stay. They won the tour 3-1 with one match drawn and as Randall made his test debut and Greig poached a hundred, they won the Calcutta test at a canter, prevailing by ten wickets on what was described as 'a poorly prepared pitch'.

Looks like Charlie Gott had roughed up the bowlers' end after all.

Waking from the Dream

On Sunday 16th May 1976 the Crook Town touring party left the Oberoi Grand for the last time. They were waved off as heroes and friends. Hotel staff, fans and Mohun Bagan officials made the leaving almost as special as the arrival. There were mixed emotions at the departure. Sadness at the end of a great adventure and happiness at the thought of a return to loved ones and familiar things. At least Bobby Agar and Steve Bell were pleased to be on their way having missed home more than most. As much was true for the unfortunate Wilf and Elsie Collingwood, returning to the security of their home after the trauma of the first day robbery and the subsequent days spent largely in the self-imposed sanctuary of the Oberoi Grand. They were all driven to the airport in the usual taxi convoy with bags full of dirty washing, gifts from their hosts and presents for loved ones back home. They also carried with them the most intangible but most valuable luggage of all, memories, pictures, encounters, magical moments that almost thirty years on would still make them smile.

The airport was awash with yet more fans, media and officials to see them safely on their journey. One last team photograph for the press. One last garland round the neck. Hand shakes, embraces and promises of lasting friendship. The team boarded the bone shaker to Bombay for the first leg of their return journey. It was unfortunate but perhaps to be expected, that the connecting flight to Heathrow was delayed because of problems with the onward flight from Hong Kong, which they were to catch. They were forced to spend the night in a Bombay airport hotel before catching a flight the following morning. There were no complaints. Everyone was too tired. The events of the previous two weeks were beginning to take their toll. There had been muted banter on the plane to Bombay but the overwhelming feeling was of exhaustion mixed with the realisation that the experience of a lifetime was over. They could no longer see a hundred thousand cheering fans, or hear the crazy sounds of the Calcutta streets. There were no cameras, no servants, no beggars, no ambassadors. They couldn't stand on a balcony and look down on the clouds or see the moon over Everest.

The following day, the tourists completed the final leg of a marathon journey back to London's Heathrow airport. The whole party was physically shattered. They'd floated through two weeks on adrenaline, high spirits, good will and kindness but now that it was over they'd hit the buffers. The Jumbo Jet taxied to a halt and the passengers disembarked wearily. The

Crook Town road show was back in England, the heroes returned. But as they made their way through customs - many of the players fearing that the bounty they had acquired in the form of gifts would mark them out as smugglers - and emerged on the other side, there was no-one. No press. No garlands. No official welcome. They were completely unknown to the people in Heathrow airport. They were anonymous. Their celebrity had disappeared as quickly, as suddenly and as unexpectedly as it had arrived. They were aircraft passengers who had just landed after a long flight – like everyone else. To further emphasise that they were back in the real world, their real world, the coach taking them onward to Crook broke down at Darlington and they had to hire taxis for the final few miles home. Welcome back to reality.

Reality was for some, a continued career in professional football. For others it was retirement. For some it was back to being a butcher, a milkman or a rigger at ICI. Tragically, midfielder Paul Brown died suddenly in his late forties but the other amateurs continued to play their football and work at their jobs. For the men who were so central to the whole Crook Town in India story, life has dealt all manner of cards from the ace to the joker. Dr. Banerjee continued as a general practitioner in Crook until retirement in June 2000 and is still as chipper and dapper as ever and working as a locum. Ronnie James worked for four more years in the stores at ATM before closure, enforced retirement and the onset of several illnesses, any one of which could floor a man. He's still fighting and still loves Crook Town. Gordon Jones gave up on football management to concentrate and expand the Teesside based newsagents business he had started as a player. You would never suspect that he too has had to battle, in his case against leukaemia. But he's winning, still smiling and is enjoying a renewed relationship with Middlesbrough FC as a match day hospitality host. Pat Partridge continued as a referee of the highest calibre until retiring to work in the family farming business in 1981. He still lives on the farm near, Cockfield but is more concerned with his charity golf appearances now.

And Bobby Charlton, the world star who nearly went to India but didn't? I'm sorry, I haven't been able to trace him though I'm told he's still involved in football.

Crook, february 2003 (Part II)

So, I'd heard it from the horse's mouth. It all sounded so straight forward. Let's organise a football tour to India. Okay, I'll do it. I just happen to be a life member of the greatest football team in India so I'll make a few phone calls. Well, that's how it appeared at first hearing. But, of course it was more complicated than that. Dr. Banerjee had been more help than I could have hoped. The story was more wonderful than I could have imagined.

I'd even learned a few things about Indian society and the Hindu religion and engaged in an interesting and illuminating conversation with Mrs. Banerjee about the caste system. But best of all, I'd been further enthused about this remarkable football tour.

"You must see my photograph album. I have many good pictures of the tour."

We leafed through the album, which brought to life many of the set piece situations described by the doctor. Leaving Heathrow, being greeted at Calcutta airport with garlands, cocktails at the ambassador's residence, lining up with the Indian President, Terry Paine making his appearance at Eden Gardens. Marvellous.

However, this was but the warm up act before the main turn. The piece de resistance was about to be unleashed on me.

"I believe I have something else that may interest you. I have a video."

"What? A video of the tour? You're kidding."

"I took some film. It's now on a video. Not many people have seen this. You may borrow it. But I must have it back next week to take to India with me."

This was too good to be true. Actual video footage of the tour. I couldn't wait to get it home.

"Well, thank you for all your help. It's been terrific. Of course I'll return the pictures and video next week. I'll watch this before I settle down to the BAFTAs tonight."

Mrs. Banerjee, who was watching Sky Sports at the time suddenly sprang into life.

"The BAFTAs? Tonight? Which channel? Oh, we can't miss the BAFTAs. There is an Indian director nominated. We'll be cheering him on."

"Oh, right. I'll look out for him. I'll tell you what. This story would make a great film. In fact, in my mind I've already cast both of you. Meera Syal and Sanjeev Bakshar. It'll be up for a BAFTA in a couple of years time."

After joking about putting them up in lights, I took my leave of the Banerjees after wishing India well in the British Academy Awards and headed back to Sedgefield in the highest spirits, convinced this was a gem of a story. I had several other people to see to flesh out the detail but this had been a most encouraging first step.

Back home, I hastened with some anticipation to the video recorder, eager to uncover the secrets of the tape that so few people had seen. A few holiday snaps perhaps? A bit of shaky video at one of the games perhaps? No. It was all there. Action footage, television interviews, meeting and greeting, wandering round the winding streets of Darjeeling above the clouds and tea plantations. But this was a picture only video. No sounds to accompany the movement. But wait. What's this? Music. Someone had thoughtfully overdubbed the footage with popular tunes from the time to give depth to the viewing. A lovely thought. And there he was. Charlie Gott, proud chin, steel in the eyes, hand on the boy shoulder of Anindo Banerjee, leading out Crook Town before one hundred thousand cheering spectators to face Mohun Bagan on the first match of this magical tour. And all to the theme tune from Hawaii Five O.

You know, people make films out of stories like this.

Oh, yes, speaking of the movies.

"The winner of the Carl Foreman award for special achievement by a director, screenwriter or producer in their first feature film is.........Asif Kapadia, for The Warriers."

The Indian director won the BAFTA for his sweeping mythical adventure set in feudal India, which resulted in a pursuit north into the Himalayan Mountains. Sound familiar?

At around 9.30pm on the 23rd February 2003, a small cheer could be heard rising from the doctor's house in Crook.

The Nag's Head
Sedgefield

A well Balanced Selection of

Home Cooked Food

Served Throughout the Week

Traditional Sunday Lunches

Served 12 - 2:30pm

Meals Served

Tues-Fri 5-9:30pm & Wed-Sat 12-2:00pm
Sat 6-9:30pm

Evening Specials   Tues- Fri 5-7:00pm

Our Resturant/Function Room

is Available for Use Throughout the Week

A Good Selection of

Real Ales and Lagers

01740 620234

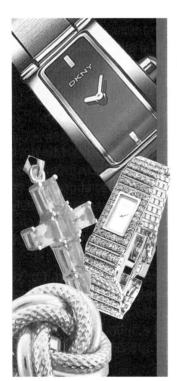

HARDWICK HALL
HOTEL

Situated in the beautiful County Durham countryside yet within easy reach of the A1 (M) and A19, Hardwick Hall provides a warm welcome to visitors who expects International standards in comfort and communications.

Bedrooms combine antique furnishings and high tech communications (ISDN and modem) including satellite, DVD, widescreen and plasma televisions.

Spacious bathrooms with huge walk in showers and deep baths offer accommodation of the highest standard, providing excellent views across the gardens and parkland of the Hardwick Country Park.

HARDWICK HALL HOTEL, SEDGEFIELD, COUNTY DURHAM. TS21 2EH

Telephone 01740 620253 Facsimile 01740 622771

www.hardwickhallhotel.co.uk   hardwickhall.sedgefield@virgin.net

there are many forms of communication, choose the right one...

MIDDLESBROUGH MUNICIPAL GOLF CENTRE

'A Course For All Seasons'

Voted one of the Top 18 Public Courses in Britain!

PAY AND PLAY, GROUPS, SOCIETIES AND CLUB BOOKINGS ALL WELCOME!!!

'A Facility for All Occasions'
Weddings, Birthdays, Anniversaries,
Business Lunches, etc. All catered for.

Alan Hope, PGA Professional, The Golf Shop and Floodlit Driving Range. Tel. M'bro 300720

Municipal Golf Centre
Ladgate Lane
Middlesbrough TS5 7YZ

**Telephone 01642 315533
Fax: 01642 300726**

Hays Travel

As the North East's Largest Independent Travel Agent we aim to offer our clients the widest choice of availabilty at the lowest prices.

We offer:

- massive discounts with all major tour operators

- Free Travel Insurance

- Free or low cost local airport taxis

AND

- 0% commission on Foreign Currency

Free insurance*

No deposit

Free or low cost transport to local airports*

MASSIVE Discounts

Lowest prices guaranteed*

Independent advice

Come into: **10 HOPE STREET, CROOK**

or call (01388) 766166

or click www.hays-travel.co.uk

Nobody offers you more!